Pension Funds and Other Institutional Investors

Pension Funds and Other Institutional Investors

Performance and Evaluation

Edward Malca
Richmond College of The
City University of New York

Lexington Books
D.C. Heath and Company
Lexington, Massachusetts
Toronto London

Library of Congress Cataloging in Publication Data

Malca, Edward.
Pension funds and other institutional investors.

Bibliography: p.
Includes index.
1. Institutional investments–United States. 2. Pension trusts–United States–Investments. I. Title.
HC4910.M28 332.6 74-14417
ISBN 0-669-95513-2

Published simultaneously in Canada.

Printed in the United States of America.

International Standard Book Number: 0-669-95513-2

Library of Congress Catalog Card Number: 74-14417

Contents

List of Figures

List of Tables

Acknowledgments

There were numerous persons and institutions who provided helpful advice, important information and valuable comments during the preparation of this book. Among them were: Dr. James L. Farrell, Jr. of the College Retirement Equities Fund; Mr. W. Moss Luy, Vice-President of Wiesenberger Services, Inc.; Mr. A. Michael Lipper, President of Lipper Analytical Services, Inc.; Mr. Steven Leuthold, Vice-President of Piper, Jaffrey and Hopwood, Inc.; Mr. Carl Whitt and Mr. Kenneth K. Mihata, both of Callan Associates. A special note of thanks goes to Mr. Gerald Murchison, Vice-President of Callan Associates, who offered extremely valuable information and fine suggestions.

I also wish to thank Professors Barry Bressler of Richmond College and Peter M. Gutmann of Baruch College for their encouragement and assistance. Mr. Ed Kazem, a graduate student at Baruch College, provided extremely valuable research assistance during the preparation of the text and the statistical tables. His endurance was appreciated. Mrs. Barbara Feldman did an excellent job of helping to edit part of this book. And very special praise goes to Mrs. Alice Egan—the perfectionist responsible for the superb typing of this manuscript.

Finally, the contributions of my wife, Jeanette, were of inestimable importance. She painstakingly edited every page of the manuscript and gave very helpful advice at every stage of this undertaking. She deserves much of the credit for whatever lucid writing can be found in these pages. This acknowledgment of my debt to her is definitely the largest understatement of all.

Edward Malca
April 15, 1975

1 Introduction

Since the late sixties, there has been an increasing scrutiny of the performance, growth, and influence of institutional investors in the stock market. Their role in the equities market has increased dramatically, while that of the individual investor has declined substantially.

A small item appeared in the *Wall Street Journal* in March 1974; the caption read: "Shareholders Total in U.S. Declined Again in 1973."[1] As if to emphasize further the decreasing role of the small investor, the following statement appeared shortly thereafter in the *New York Times*:

> (Stock) holdings of pension funds, investment companies, insurance companies, nonprofit organizations, common trust funds and mutual savings banks increased to 31.4% of the Big Board (NYSE) list in 1973 from 30.8% at the end of 1972.[2]

Furthermore, total institutional investor ownership of New York Stock Exchange (NYSE) companies is approximately 45 percent when the following institutions are included: bank-administered personal trust funds, hedge funds, investment counselors, nonbank trusts, foreign-based institutional investors, and nonregistered mutual funds.[3]

Thus, while the number of individual investors has diminished from 32.5 million in 1971 to 30.9 million in 1973, the role of the institutional investor has increased from 35 percent of NYSE daily volume in 1963 to an estimated 73 percent in early 1974.[4] The ever-increasing importance of these institutions in the stock market and in our economy has generated much greater concern as to their activities and performance.

In fact, during the early 1970s many congressional committees have held hearings on the role of these financial institutions in the economy.[5] These hearings are particularly concerned with the impact of these intermediaries upon our financial markets. Do they, indeed, have a beneficial effect upon the efficient allocation of financial resources?[6]

Institutional Investor Assets

Table 1-1 shows the astronomical increase in assets and common stock holdings of institutional investors. Private noninsured pension fund assets increased from $18 billion in 1955 to over $150 billion in 1972—an increase of more than 800 percent. State and local retirement funds enjoyed a similar rise in assets from $11 billion in 1955 to over $80 billion in 1973. Furthermore, the stock portfolios of private noninsured pension funds increased from $5.5 billion in 1955 to $111.8 billion in 1972, that is, an overwhelming 2,000 percent increase in less than two decades. In contrast, the stock holdings of investment companies increased a respectable but relatively smaller 550 percent from $11.5 billion to $64 billion during the same period. As indicated previously, institutional investors own 45 percent of all NYSE listed stocks.[7]

Financial intermediaries have risen to such prominence in the last two decades because they have provided a service that fits the needs of individuals. In the case of mutual funds, the individual is purchasing both a diversified portfolio and professional asset management.[8] With pension funds, the employer usually contributes to the pension in the name of the employees (tax-free to employees now). These funds are usually administered by a bank trust department whose goal is generally the maximization of long-term growth of these pension assets. Among the many reasons for the rise of pension funds is the tax deductibility of contributions by the employer, while taxable to the employee upon retirement, generally at a lower tax rate. Here, too, the individual gets professional investment management and tax advantages, while he gives up current income for deferred compensation, which hopefully will be increased by growth of the pension assets.

Thus, the increased growth of financial intermediaries has been due to their ability to fill the needs of a large segment of the population. With increased affluence, the likelihood of further specialization of investment management seems quite probable.

Concentration of Assets

Institutional demand for common stocks has been quite strong during the last 15 years. This demand, no doubt, has had a considerable effect upon the stock market, especially since 1958 when aggregate purchases of common stocks by financial institutions exceeded net new corporate equity issues for the first time. As indicated in Table 1-2, each year since 1958 these institutions have purchased a greater amount of common stocks than were issued. This factor alone should have increased the importance of these institutions in the stock market.

The New York Stock Exchange has documented the steadily increasing importance of the institutional investor upon the equities market. As indicated in Table 1-3, institutions owned less than 16 percent of NYSE-listed stocks in 1956, whereas, less than 20 years later in 1973, this ownership increased to 31.4 percent.[9]

In discussing institutional investors, one must keep in mind that private noninsured pension funds are, by far, the largest institutional investors in the stock market today. In 1956 these pension funds owned 2.4 percent of all stocks traded on the New York Stock Exchange while in 1972 this figure was 11 percent.[10] It has been estimated that at the beginning of 1974 this figure was probably 12 percent.[11]

It must also be kept in mind that most of these institutional funds are managed by a relatively few financial intermediaries. As can be seen in Table 1-4, as of the end of 1972 there were 32 institutional investors managing over $300 billion. This concentration is further accentuated by the fact that, for the largest institutional investor, an investment committee of eight men makes the final investment decision that affects $21 billion in common stock.[12]

It is apparent from Table 1-4 that the largest concentration of institutional assets is, by far, in bank trust departments. In fact, the latest Federal Deposit Insurance Corporation (FDIC) estimate is that all bank trust departments manage $404 billion of assets.[13] For this reason trust departments are examined in greater detail in later chapters. Unfortunately, until Congress passes a full disclosure bill, a complete analysis and understanding of trust department activities will not be possible.[14]

The fact that the largest 20 banks control 48 percent of all United States trust and pension assets further emphasizes the huge concentration of assets.[15] Furthermore, the two largest bank trust departments manage more stocks and bonds than all of the 500 mutual funds in the United States combined.[16] Further illustrating the concentration of financial assets as of mid-1973 is the fact that the

Table 1-1
Total Assets and Common Stockholdings of Institutional Investors (in Billions of Dollars; at Market Value; End of Year

	1955	1956	1957	1958	1959	1960	1961	1962	1963	1964	1965	1966	1967	1968	1969	1970	1971	1972	1973
Private noninsured pension plans																			
Assets	18.1	20.0	22.7	28.2	32.4	37.1	45.3	46.7	54.6	63.9	72.9	72.8	85.5	96.0	94.6	104.7	126.9	154.3	129.9
Common stock	5.5	6.4	6.8	10.8	13.8	15.8	22.1	21.2	26.9	33.0	40.0	38.7	50.1	60.1	59.8	65.5	86.6	113.4	88.0
Investment companies[a]																			
Assets	13.8	16.1	15.0	21.6	25.1	23.8	33.5	31.0	35.8	40.8	47.0	45.3	58.4	69.5	61.8	61.5	72.3	79.8	66.2
Common stock	11.5	13.5	12.2	18.3	21.3	19.8	28.3	25.6	30.2	34.7	40.0	36.2	49.2	57.0	49.8	48.5	57.9	64.0	48.9
Life insurance companies[b]																			
Assets	90.4	96.0	101.3	107.6	113.6	119.6	126.8	133.3	141.1	149.5	158.9	167.5	177.8	188.6	197.2	207.3	222.1	239.7	252.4
Common stock	1.9	2.0	1.9	2.5	3.0	3.2	4.2	4.1	4.8	5.4	6.3	6.0	7.8	10.0	10.3	11.9	16.8	21.8	19.6
Property and liability insurance companies[c]																			
Assets	21.7	22.5	22.8	25.7	27.9	29.4	32.9	33.5	37.1	39.9	41.8	42.3	46.6	51.2	52.4	58.6	67.3	78.9	80.7
Common stock[d]	4.6	4.8	4.4	5.9	6.4	6.7	8.5	7.8	9.0	10.4	10.9	9.9	11.7	13.2	11.9	11.7	14.6	18.9	16.3

Personal trust funds																			
Assets	48.7	50.0	45.5	55.6	61.9	63.3	75.1	74.8	88.6	91.3	98.4	96.6	108.0	118.0	113.3	114.8	134.5	153.2	140.0
Common stock	27.8	30.3	27.4	36.7	40.8	41.6	52.9	49.6	58.9	62.1	68.0	65.1	74.2	81.4	77.2	76.1	91.2	107.0	92.5
Common trust funds																			
Assets	1.9	2.0	2.0	2.4	2.7	2.8	3.6	4.5	4.5	5.8	7.5	7.6	8.3	9.6	9.2	10.1	12.7	15.2	14.2
Common stock	0.9	1.0	0.9	1.3	1.4	1.5	2.0	1.8	2.2	2.8	3.3	3.1	3.7	4.6	4.3	4.3	5.4	7.1	6.0
Mutual savings banks																			
Assets	31.3	33.4	35.2	37.8	38.9	40.6	42.8	46.1	49.7	54.2	58.2	61.0	66.4	71.2	74.2	79.0	89.6	100.6	106.6
Common stock	0.5	0.5	0.6	0.6	0.6	0.5	0.7	0.8	0.9	0.9	1.0	1.0	1.2	1.4	1.6	1.8	2.1	2.5	2.8
State and local retirement funds																			
Assets	10.7	12.1	13.8	15.3	17.3	19.6	22.0	24.5	26.9	29.7	33.1	37.4	41.5	46.3	51.4	57.7	64.5	71.5	78.7
Common stock	0.1	0.1	0.2	0.2	0.3	0.4	0.5	0.7	0.9	1.1	1.4	1.9	2.6	3.8	5.5	7.6	10.8	13.7	17.3
Foundations																			
Assets	18.1	18.6	18.1	18.8	20.7	20.8	23.0	23.4	24.5	27.0	28.7	28.3	29.9	31.5	29.5	32.0	36.5	39.5	36.0
Common stock	11.0	11.6	11.0	12.0	13.4	13.1	14.8	13.9	15.1	17.3	19.1	18.3	19.8	21.6	19.6	21.6	24.5	28.0	24.1
Educational endowments																			
Assets	4.8	5.5	5.4	6.5	7.2	7.3	8.6	8.3	9.4	10.5	11.7	11.1	13.1	13.6	13.0	13.0	14.3	16.2	14.5
Common stock	2.8	3.1	2.9	3.8	4.1	4.0	4.9	4.4	5.4	6.1	6.9	6.1	7.6	8.0	7.4	7.7	8.9	10.6	8.8

[a]Includes open-end, closed-end, face amount, and unit trust.

[b]Includes separate accounts; statement value.

[c]Statement value.

[d]Excludes holdings of insurance company stock.

Source: Securities and Exchange Commission, *Statistical Bulletin*, August 1973 and August 1974, p. 808 and p. 865, respectively.

Table 1-2
Net Purchases and Sales of Corporate Stocks, 1950-73

Year	Net New Issues Of Corporate Stocks[a]	Net Purchase of Stocks by: Financial Institutions[b]	Individuals[c]	Foreigners	Excess Institutional Purchases Over Net New Issues
		(In Billions of Dollars)			
1973	$ 8.5	$ 9.7	$ 5.2	$ 4.0	$ 1.2
1972	13.0	16.2	5.5	2.3	3.2
1971	13.5	17.9	−5.3	0.9	4.4
1970	6.8	11.1	−5.0	0.7	4.3
1969	4.2	12.6	−10.0	1.6	8.4
1968	−0.9	10.0	−12.9	2.0	10.9
1967	2.3	9.1	−7.5	0.7	6.8
1966	1.1	5.9	−4.5	−0.3	4.8
1965	0.0	5.7	−5.3	−0.4	5.7
1964	1.4	3.9	−2.2	−0.3	2.5
1963	−0.2	3.4	−3.8	0.2	3.6
1962	0.7	4.2	−3.6	0.1	3.5
1961	2.6	4.3	−2.0	0.3	1.7
1960	1.7	3.5	−2.0	0.2	1.8
1959	2.4	3.3	−1.3	0.4	0.9
1958	2.1	2.8	−0.6	−0.1	0.7
1957	2.7	2.2	0.4	0.1	−0.5
1956	2.5	1.7	0.5	0.3	−0.8
1955	1.9	1.6	0.2	0.1	−0.3
1954	1.8	1.6	0.1	0.1	−0.2
1953	1.9	1.3	0.5	0.1	−0.6
1952	2.4	1.4	1.0	0.0	−1.0
1951	2.3	0.7	1.5	0.1	−1.6
1950	1.5	1.0	0.5	0.0	−0.5

[a]Gross new corporate cash offerings (common and preferred) plus stock options, all other sales and bond conversions, less cash retirements and merger exchanges into bonds.

[b]Net stock purchases by mutual savings banks, life insurance companies, fire and casualty companies, private noninsured pension funds, state and local government retirement funds, and open-end mutual funds. Excludes personal trust accounts at banks.

[c]The figure for net individual purchases and sales is a residual calculation, and is significantly less reliable than some of the other figures. Since mutual fund purchases of equities are included in the institutional category, individuals' purchases of mutual fund shares are not included.

Source: Securities and Exchange Commission, *Statistical Bulletin*; and Federal Reserve System, *Federal Reserve Bulletin*, December 1974, pp. A58, A59.

Table 1-3
Estimated Holdings of New York Stock Exchange-listed Stocks by Selected Institutional Investors (in Billions of Dollars)

	Year End				
Type of Institution	1949	1962	1971	1972	1973 p[a]
Insurance companies					
Life	$ 1.1	$ 4.1	$ 16.1	$ 21.2	$ 21.1
Nonlife	1.7	7.1	15.6	18.6	16.9
Investment companies					
Open-end	1.4	15.4	46.7	51.4	37.2
Closed-end	1.6	5.3	5.6	6.4	5.0
Noninsured pension funds					
Corporate	0.5	17.9	75.6	98.6	82.2
Other private	b	1.0	4.6	5.9	4.9
State and local government	b	0.6	10.7	13.6	15.5
Nonprofit institutions					
Foundations	2.5	8.5	19.3	23.9	19.2
Educational endowments	1.1	3.5	7.4	8.8	7.5
Other	1.0	5.0	10.1	11.8	9.5
Common trust funds	b	1.7	5.5	6.8	5.5
Mutual savings banks	0.2	0.4	1.5	1.5	1.7
Total	$11.1	$ 70.5	$218.7	$268.5	$226.2
Market value of all NYSE-listed stock	$76.3	$345.8	$741.8	$871.5	$721.0
Estimated percent held by above institutions	14.5%	20.4%	29.5%	30.8%	31.4%

[a]p = preliminary estimates. Prior data have been revised.

[b]Less than $50 million.

Source: New York Stock Exchange, *1974 Fact Book*, June 1974, p. 52.

10 largest bank trust departments held almost 30 percent of Polaroid and Xerox and nearly 40 percent of Walt Disney.[17]

Notwithstanding the potential and actual economic power implied in this concentration, the emphasis in this study is upon the ability of these financial institutions to administer satisfactorily the funds entrusted to them. Perhaps the excessive concentration in a select few equity issues, as mentioned previously, raises serious questions as to the degree of risk associated with such a concentration. As stated by Senator Bentsen during recent hearings of his Senate Subcommit-

Table 1-4
Thirty-two Institutional Investors with Assets Under Management of $5 Billion and Over, End of Year 1972

	Billions
1. Morgan Guaranty Trust Company	$27.4
2. Bankers Trust Company, New York	19.9
3. Prudential Insurance Company of America	18.3
4. First National City Bank, New York	17.2
5. U.S. Trust Company of New York	17.0
6. Metropolitan Life Insurance Company	16.5
7. Equitable Life Assurance Society	16.4
8. Chase Manhattan Bank	16.2
9. Travelers Corporation	13.1
10. New York Life Insurance Company	11.5
11. Manufacturers Hanover Trust Company	10.9
12. Mellon National Bank and Trust Company	10.5
13. Investors Diversified Services	9.7
14. First National Bank of Chicago	8.4
15. Continental Illinois National Bank & Trust Co.	8.2
16. Aetna Life and Casualty Group	8.2
17. Scudder, Stevens and Clark	7.2
18. Bank of America	7.1
19. Harris Trust and Savings Bank	7.0
20. Wilmington Trust Company	7.0
21. First National Bank of Boston	6.8
22. Northern Trust Company, Chicago	6.7
23. Chemical Bank, New York	6.5
24. National Bank of Detroit	6.5
25. Loomis, Sayles and Company	6.3
26. Northwestern Mutual Life Insurance Company	6.1
27. Lionel D. Edie and Company	6.1
28. Wells Fargo Bank	6.0
29. Equitable Trust Company of Baltimore	5.5
30. Girard Bank, Philadelphia	5.2
31. Crocker Citizens National Bank	5.0
32. Security Pacific National Bank	5.0

Source: U.S., Congress, Senate, Subcommittee on Intergovernmental Relations of the Committee on Government Operation, March 4, 1974, *Disclosure of Corporate Ownership* (Washington, D.C.: U.S. Government Printing Office, 1974) p. 1.

tee on Financial Markets, "the main concern is . . . that hard-earned funds which are being invested by professional managers are adequately protected."[18]

Moreover, the proper functioning and investing by these institutions are imperatives for the efficient allocation of financial resources. As Dr. Ture stated before the Senate Subcommittee on Financial Markets:

> A . . . function of financial markets is to facilitate the efficient allocation of saving. In brief, the condition for efficient allocation of saving is that, at the margin, the present value of the future income contributed by every dollar of saving is the same (when adjustment is made for differences in risk). In an efficiently operating financial market, information about a company performance and prospects is quickly translated into valuation of the equity interest in companies and changes in these relative valuations are cues to savers-investors as to changes in the composition of their investments which they can make in order to maximize the future income they can realize from their saving.
>
> . . . Impediments to effective performance by financial markets, therefore, also prevent the most efficient allocation and use of the economy's resources, which means that the economy . . . is deprived of valuable output which it otherwise would enjoy. Efficient financial markets, therefore, are important concern for all of us. . . .[19]

As Dr. Ture has aptly stated, a less than efficient financial market will be detrimental not only to those in the market, but, more importantly, to our entire economy. Thus, such intense concentration by large institutions in a few companies, unless justified by performance, may signify an inefficient allocation of financial resources. In fact, due to such concentration, some experts are calling for the break-up of the largest 10 to 20 investment management firms.[20]

This extensive concentration of financial resources in the hands of relatively few institutions may be justified if these large institutions are, indeed, the best administrators of these funds. Moreover, if the concentration of these assets in a small number of equity securities provides the best results, then this investment philosophy may have significant merit. In addition, if economies of scale exist in the investment field, then these large pools of assets may prove acceptable.

One of the main purposes of this study is to determine whether the institutional administrators of investment funds are adequately and efficiently managing these hundreds of billions of dollars in assets. Another aspect of this analysis determines whether or not the goals these institutions sell to their clients are actually achieved. This information is crucial to an efficient allocation of financial resources, and thus to our entire economy.

Financial Institution's Stock Holdings

The last two decades witnessed an astronomical increase in the importance and the assets of financial institutions. This was accompanied by a dramatic change toward equity investing in their portfolio composition. Table 1-5 illustrates the fact that common stocks have become an increasingly important component of institutional portfolios. Of particular interest is the fact that over 70 percent of the assets of noninsured pension funds were invested in corporate stock in 1973, while less than 15 years ago this figure was below 40 percent. During this period, these institutions were growing

Table 1-5
Corporate Stocks as Percent of Total Assets, 1952-73

Year End	Investment Companies	Noninsured Pension Funds	Life Insurance Companies	Other Insurance Companies	State and Local Retirement Funds	Mutual Savings Banks
1973	82.3%	66.9%	10.6%	28.5%	22.8%	3.8%
1972	86.4	73.4	11.5	32.3	20.4	3.6
1971	85.6	67.4	9.6	28.4	17.3	3.3
1970	83.3	60.7	7.7	26.5	13.8	3.2
1969	84.6	60.1	7.2	29.2	11.5	2.9
1968	87.5	60.6	7.2	32.6	8.9	2.7
1967	87.6	57.1	6.3	31.8	6.7	2.5
1966	83.1	52.1	5.4	29.6	5.7	2.4
1965	87.6	55.4	5.9	32.9	4.9	2.4
1964	88.1	52.4	5.5	32.7	4.2	2.3
1963	87.6	50.0	5.2	30.8	3.7	2.3
1962	86.2	46.3	4.9	28.7	3.2	2.3
1961	88.5	49.4	5.1	31.9	2.7	2.1
1960	87.0	43.3	4.3	28.4	2.2	2.0
1959	87.7	42.6	4.1	28.7	2.0	2.1
1958	88.2	39.5	3.9	29.0	1.8	2.3
1957	85.0	32.0	3.5	25.1	1.5	2.2
1956	87.2	33.6	3.8	27.8	1.3	2.1
1955	88.4	33.3	4.1	27.7	1.2	2.1
1954	87.8	22.9	4.0	25.5	1.0	1.9
1953	84.9	20.6	3.4	21.3	.9	1.6
1952	84.6	19.2	3.4	22.7	.8	1.3

Source: Division of Research and Statistics, Federal Reserve System, June 1972 *Flow of Funds Accounts*; and Federal Reserve System, *Federal Reserve Bulletin*, October 1974, p. A59.25.

at a rate greater than 20 percent annually. Other institutions that are especially noteworthy are the life insurance companies and state and local retirement funds. In recent years both have put a major emphasis upon common stock investing. Equities represented over 10 percent of life insurance portfolios in 1973, while only 10 years earlier they comprised 5 percent. More importantly, state and local retirement funds are steadily increasing their investments in common stocks. This can be shown by the fact that in 1963 equities represented less than 4 percent of their total portfolio while 10 years later more than 20 percent of their assets were invested in common stock. This greatly increased emphasis upon equities is of notable importance since state and local retirement funds are among the fastest growing financial institutions today.

A more dramatic illustration of the changed attitude toward common stock investing is represented in Table 1-6, showing the amount of new net annual asset increases (cash flow) devoted to equity purchases. As can be seen, all major institutional categories except mutual funds, which have traditionally kept a large percentage of common stock, have consistently been increasing the portion of cash flow directed to net equity purchases.

Most experts in the field foresee further institutionalization of equity markets in the years ahead. A recent study by Professor Robert M. Soldofsky predicted that this trend will continue, and that by the year 2000 financial institutions will own 55 percent of the market value of all common stocks.[21] In light of recent trends that may be a conservative estimate. Soldofsky further projects that noninsured corporate pension funds are expected to be the largest single category of equity holders, with $2.3 trillion or 26 percent of the total market value of all common stocks expected to be outstanding in the year 2000. Again, this estimate may be on the conservative side, for these pensions now own 12 percent of all NYSE stocks and are already the largest single category of common stockholders.

Significantly, Soldofsky predicts that at the end of this century institutional investors will own one-third to one-half of the stock in thousands of companies. In fact, at this time institutions already own one-third of the stock in dozens of companies. Table 1-7 summarizes Soldofsky's projections.

The principal motivation in the growing shift to equities was to increase the total return of the portfolio. The assumption was that

Table 1-6
Changes in Attitude Toward Stock Investing (in Billions of Dollars)

	1965	1966	1967	1968	1969	1970	1971	1972	1973
Private pension funds									
Net acquisition of financial assets	5.5	7.2	6.6	6.4	6.3	7.1	7.3	6.8	7.7
Net purchases of corporate equities	3.1	3.7	4.6	4.7	5.4	4.6	8.9	7.1	5.3
Net purchases of corporate equities as percent increase of net acquisitions	56.4%	51.4%	69.7%	73.4%	84.7%	64.8%	121.9%	104.4%	68.8%
State and local retirement funds									
Net acquisition of financial assets	3.3	4.2	4.1	4.8	5.5	6.3	6.3	7.9	9.4
Net purchases of corporate equities	0.4	0.5	0.7	1.3	1.8	2.1	3.2	3.5	3.9
Net purchases of corporate equities as percent increase of net acquisitions	12.1%	11.9%	17.1%	27.1%	32.7%	33.3%	50.8%	44.3%	41.5%
Life insurance companies									
Net acquisition of financial assets	8.7	8.2	8.7	9.8	9.2	9.9	12.7	15.0	16.6
Net purchase of corporate equities	0.7	0.3	1.0	1.4	1.7	2.0	3.6	3.5	3.6
Net purchases of corporate equities as percent increase of net acquisitions	8.0%	3.7%	11.5%	14.3%	18.5%	20.2%	28.3%	23.3%	21.7%

Other insurance companies									
Net acquisition of financial assets	1.2	2.1	2.0	3.1	2.9	5.5	6.6	7.9	5.6
Net purchases of corporate equities	0.1	0.4	0.3	0.8	1.0	1.0	2.5	3.0	2.2
Net purchases of corporate equities as percent increase of net acquisitions	8.3%	19.0%	15.0%	25.8%	34.5%	18.2%	37.9%	38.0%	39.3%
Mutual funds									
Net acquisition of financial assets	2.2	2.5	1.5	3.6	2.6	1.7	0.6	–1.8	–2.2
Net purchases of corporate equities	1.3	1.0	1.9	2.5	1.7	1.2	0.4	–1.8	–2.3
Net purchases of corporate equities as percent increase of net acquisitions	59.1%	40.0%	126.6%	69.4%	65.4%	70.6%	66.7%	--	--
Mutual savings banks									
Net acquisition of financial assets	4.0	2.8	5.4	4.6	3.1	4.7	10.4	11.0	6.0
Net purchases of corporate equities	0.2	--	0.2	0.3	0.2	.3	0.5	0.6	.4
Net purchases of corporate equities as percent increase of net acquisitions	5.0%	--	3.7%	6.5%	6.5%	6.4%	4.8%	5.5%	6.7%

Source: Federal Reserve System, *Federal Reserve Bulletin*, October 1974, pp. 59.10-59.12.

Table 1-7
Projected Market Value of Stockholdings of Financial Institutions

Financial Institutions	Market Value (in Billions of Dollars) 1968	1980	2000	Percentage of Total Market Value 1968	1980	2000	Growth Rates (% per Year) 1968-80	1981-2000
Noninsured corporate pension funds	$ 56.0	$269	$2,362	7.3	13.7	25.8	14.0	11.5
Investment companies	59.6	258	1,730	7.8	13.1	18.9	13.0	10.0
State and local pension pension funds	4.8	37	357	0.6	1.9	3.9	17.0	12.0
Life insurance companies	12.8	46	171	1.7	2.3	1.8	13.5	6.8
Property and casualty insurance companies	14.7	37	118	1.9	1.9	1.3	8.0	6.0
University and college endowments	9.0	28	190	1.2	1.4	2.1	10.0	10.0
Foundations	15.8	28	74	2.1	1.4	0.8	5.0	5.0
Common trust funds	4.4	11	53	0.6	0.6	0.6	9.0	8.0
Total institutional holdings	$177.1	$714	$5,055	23.2	36.3	55.2	12.3	10.3
Market value of all outstanding stock[a]	$761.3	$1.966	$9,161				8.0	8.0

[a]For widely held companies only; includes both common and preferred stocks.

Source: Robert M. Soldofsky, *Institutional Holdings of Common Stock 1900-2000*, Michigan Business Studies, vol. 18, no. 3 (Ann Arbor Michigan: Bureau of Business Research, Graduate School of Business Administration, University of Michigan, 1971), p. 209.

fixed-income securities, in the long run, were at a particular disadvantage in performance terms to common stock investing. That is, common stocks were assumed to be a better hedge against inflation than bonds. (See Table 1-8 for a demonstration of equities as an inflation hedge.) Furthermore, with the ability to diversify their common stock portfolio and without significant liquidity needs on the part of most of these financial institutions, equity investing became quite attractive, offering the lure of a greater rate of return.

The major emphasis in the remainder of this study is a thorough analysis of institutional investment performance, with special emphasis upon noninsured pension funds. Some of the questions that are investigated include: What are the investment goals of the various financial institutions? Have they been achieved? Is equity investing providing the return that these institutions expected? Are the risks taken by these institutions warranted? Do institutional investors outperform or underperform the market? How could substantial pension asset losses affect corporate profits? Is the allocation of financial resources at an optimum level?

These and many other pertinent questions are explored in the following chapters. Naturally, these matters are of importance to institutional investors; however, they are also crucial to corporations and to the 30 million workers covered by pension funds, as well as to the well-being of the economy. From a public policy point of view, the examination of institutional performance will be most important in order to determine whether an efficient allocation of financial resources has taken place.

Table 1-8
Relative Rates of Real Return: Stocks Versus Bonds

	Annual Investment Performance of S & P 500 Stock Price Index[a]	Total Return: Fixed Income Securities[b]		Consumer Price Index		Indication of Real Return		
		Aa Rated Utility Bonds	U.S. Government Bonds	Annual Level	Percent Change	S & P 500 Performance Minus CPI Increase	Aa Bond Return Minus CPI Increase	U.S. Government Bond Return Minus CPI Increase
1952	+18.26%	+3.54%	+2.58%	79.5	+2.2%	+16.0%	+1.3%	+0.4%
1953	−1.05	+3.53	+3.42	80.1	+0.8	−1.9	+2.7	+1.7
1954	+52.12	+5.99	+7.26	80.5	+0.5	+51.6	+5.5	+6.8
1955	+31.35	−0.93	−1.36	80.2	−0.4	+31.7	−0.5	−1.8
1956	+6.57	−9.88	−5.39	81.4	+1.5	+5.1	−11.4	−6.9
1957	−10.80	+9.74	+7.31	84.3	+3.6	−14.4	+6.1	+3.7
1958	+44.61	−6.52	−6.04	86.6	+2.7	+41.9	−9.2	−8.7
1959	+11.90	−3.45	−4.78	87.3	+0.8	+11.1	−4.3	+4.0
1960	+0.45	+10.45	+14.28	88.7	+1.6	−1.1	+8.9	+12.7
1961	+26.79	+2.25	−0.60	89.6	+1.0	+25.8	+1.3	−1.6
1962	−8.74	+9.31	+7.96	90.6	+1.1	−9.8	+8.2	+6.9
1963	+22.66	+0.69	−0.47	91.7	+1.2	+21.5	−0.5	−1.7
1964	+16.32	+4.39	+4.14	92.9	+1.3	+15.0	+3.1	+2.8
1965	+12.35	−1.83	−0.28	94.5	+1.7	+10.7	−0.1	−2.0
1966	−10.05	−1.08	+3.11	97.2	+2.9	−13.0	−4.0	+0.2

1967	+23.88	−8.13	−7.87	100.0	+2.9	+21.0	−11.0	−10.8
1968	+10.98	+1.88	−0.15	104.2	+4.2	+6.8	−2.3	−4.3
1969	−8.42	−9.59	−5.06	109.8	+5.4	−13.8	−15.0	−10.5
1970	+3.93	+19.45	+11.82	116.3	+5.9	−2.0	+13.6	+5.8
1971	+14.26	+9.83	+13.00	121.3	+4.3	+10.0	+5.5	+8.7
1972	+19.00	+7.00[c]	+6.00	125.3	+3.3	+15.7	+3.7	+2.7
1973	−15.00	+1.00[c]	0.00	133.1	+6.2	−21.2	−5.2	−6.2
Average annual return:								
1952-71						+10.6%	Nil	+0.3%
1952-56						+20.5	−0.5%	Nil
1957-61						+12.6	+0.6	+2.0
1962-66						+4.9	+1.3	+1.2
1967-71						+4.4	−1.8	−2.2
1969-73						−2.26	+0.05	+0.01

[a]Includes price changes and dividend payments.

[b]Total bond return equals change in price during the year plus income as percent of market price at start of year.

Aa rated utility bonds: 2-3/4%/1985 to 1965, then 4-1/4%/1991.
1950-58 2-1/2%/1967-72
1959-65 3-1/2%/1999
1966-73 4-1/4%/1987-92

[c]For 1972 and 1973, refers to high-grade, long-term corporate bonds.

Sources: Federal Reserve System, *Federal Reserve Bulletin,* October 1974, pp. A29-A31, A55; U.S. Department of Commerce, *Business Statistics 1971*, p. 40; Calculations by the author.

2 Goals and Objectives of Institutional Investors

At a corporate pension fund conference sponsored by a leading Wall Street institutional investment firm, the question of goals for pension fund performance was discussed. It was quite common, at that 1969 conference, for many participants to feel that a 15 to 20 percent return on their equity investment was a realistic and attainable goal.[1] In fact, at that session the treasurer of Scott Paper Company stated that 15 percent was the minimum expected return based upon recent stock market history.[2] Another leading figure at the conference, the president of Moody's Alliance Capital Corporation, investment advisors, flatly stated that he expected to do 5 to 10 percent better than the market averages over a period of years.[3]

At the following year's conference the market seemed to sober some of the predictions and it was found that these analysts' performance expectations were reduced but still considerably high. The expectation for a 15 to 20 percent return was generally diminished to a somewhat more realistic 12 to 15 percent return on equity investments.[4] However, the senior vice-president of one of the leading New York City banks remarked that a 15 percent return on equity investments was quite reasonable for the one- to four-year time horizon.[5] He qualified this statement by saying that a 15 percent return could not be sustained on a 15 to 20 year basis, but that a 10 to 12 percent return should be expected.[6] Moreover, he revealed that in pursuit of this goal, one third of all his bank trust department equity commitments were in just five growth stocks. The consensus of the conference participants still maintained that a good fund manager could definitely do better than the averages with a minimum long-run return of 10 to 12 percent.

There was a pervasive delusion throughout the investment community that above-average equity performance was not only possible, but was the sign of a superior fund manager. As one West Coast banker explained, the objective of his pooled equity fund was "to seek above average return on invested capital . . . with reasonable risk limitations."[7] Or, as a Midwest banker stated in reference to his bank's pooled equity funds accounts: "The goal of the fund is above average growth with a total return exceeding the generally recognized common stock averages."[8]

The investment managers and their clients generally believed that it was not only possible but very likely that these above-average equity performances would be achieved. However, as discussed in subsequent chapters, these performance projections were generally not attained.

This euphoric attitude towards equity performance was quite understandable, given the recent history at that time. It was a period when the high growth ("go-go") mutual funds were promising and achieving, for a short time, performance results of 25 to 50 percent per annum.[9] Other institutions, especially pensions, were looking at these funds and enviously envisioning the prospects of a 15 to 20 percent equity return, which would very favorably affect pension contributions. It has been estimated by the Federal Reserve that as little as a 1/4 percent increase in pension performance would decrease corporate contributions by over 8 percent.[10] Thus, corporations dreamed of the possibility of reducing pension contributions by 25 to 50 percent because of increased equity performance.

The decade of the seventies has been, so far, a truly sobering experience for the investment community.

At a recent Institutional Investor conference, it was a rare fund manager indeed who thought that he could out-perform the market.[11] Most agreed that they would be doing satisfactorily if their equity performance matched the Standard and Poor's 500 Stock Index.[12] Thus, the investment community has come almost full circle in just five years—from its earlier performance cult to its present-day objective of doing as well as the market.

The remainder of this chapter is devoted to an analysis of the objectives of institutional investors as evidenced by their stated goals and actuarial assumptions. Pension funds are also analyzed, with special emphasis upon their rapid growth, contributions, size, influence, and importance in the economy. Moreover, the long-term relative performance of equity investments is discussed and compared with the equity performance objectives of institutional investors. In subsequent chapters, an in-depth analysis of the performance of different institutional investors is presented.

In discussing the institutional investor, one must keep in mind that private noninsured pension funds are, by far, the largest institutional investor in the stock market today. Each year this group purchases more common stocks than all other institutional investors combined. In fact, as can be seen in Table 2-1, private noninsured pension funds accounted for well over 60 percent of all stock purchases by financial institutions. These pension funds have dominated equity purchases for the last decade.

In order to obtain a better understanding of private noninsured pension funds today, one must first comprehend the rapid growth that has taken place since World War II. As can be seen in Table 2-2, the growth of these pensions has been quite substantial. In 1950 they had assets of less than $5 billion, while just 22 years later they mushroomed to over $154 billion (at market value). This represents a growth of over 3,000 percent in this period. Due to substantial stock market reversals in 1973, their assets have been reduced to under $130 billion at market value.[13] The assets declined by $31 billion, which includes the loss of $7 billion that was contributed into the funds in 1973.[14] It is quite likely that for the year 1974 the market value of pension assets has also declined dramatically, even in light of increased contributions into these funds. In fact, the following data illustrate the extremely poor equity performance achieved by pension funds in 1973 (1974 data is not presently available). At market value pensions held $113.4 billion of common stocks in 1972, which was decreased over $25 billion to $88 billion at the end of 1973.[15] This occurred in spite of net stock purchases of $5.5 billion for that same year. Thus, their equity losses for 1973 were over $30 billion, representing 25 percent of their total equity portfolio. The results for pension equity investing in 1974 have not yet been disclosed, although in Chapter 3 performance studies of pooled pensions includes some data through June 30, 1974. However, it seems likely at this writing that a poor performance similar to that of 1973 has occurred.

One major advantage that pensions have over most other financial institutions is their steady and generally increasing net inflow of funds each year. These net receipts are the main reason why forced liquidations and liquidity are not a present problem of pension. Their obligations are long term, 20 to 30 years, and fairly predictable. Also, contributions to the funds far exceed the benefits paid. This is quite an enviable position for a financial institution. In fact, it seems quite probable that these pensions will have a net inflow of funds for the foreseeable future.

Table 2-1
Common Stock Transaction and Activity Rates of Selected Financial Institutions

	1965	1966	1967	1968	1969	1970	1971	1972	1973
Private noninsured pension funds[a]									
Purchases	5,585	6,610	10,035	12,285	15,230	13,955	21,685	23,220	20,325
Sales	2,560	3,165	5,655	7,815	10,270	9,370	12,800	15,650	14,790
Net purchases	3,025	3,445	4,380	4,470	4,960	4,585	8,885	7,570	5,535
Activity rate	11.4	12.6	17.2	18.7	21.3	20.5	22.1	19.7	16.5
Open-end investment companies[b]									
Purchases	6,530	10,365	14,925	20,100	22,060	17,130	21,555	20,945	15,560
Sales	5,165	9,320	13,325	18,495	19,850	15,900	21,175	22,550	17,505
Net purchases	1,365	1,045	1,600	1,605	2,205	1,225	380	−1,610	−1,945
Activity rate	21.8	34.0	40.7	48.4	51.0	45.6	48.2	44.8	39.0
Life insurance companies[c]									
Purchases	985	1,110	1,685	2,930	3,705	3,770	6,230	6,910	6,320
Sales	600	825	875	1,725	2,185	1,975	2,775	4,425	4,035
Net purchases	390	285	805	1,205	1,520	1,795	3,455	2,485	2,290
Activity rate	13.8	16.0	18.2	26.8	29.4	27.8	31.0	29.6	24.8

Property-liability insurance companies									
Purchases	770	900	1,165	2,245	3,780	3,615	4,170	5,130	4,520
Sales	965	825	980	1,645	2,880	2,720	1,945	2,740	2,855
Net purchases	–190	80	185	600	900	890	2,225	2,390	1,665
Activity rate	8.2	8.6	9.7	16.0	26.7	28.1	23.2	23.8	20.3
Total selected institutions									
Purchases	13,875	18,985	27,810	37,565	44,775	38,465	53,645	56,205	46,725
Sales	9,285	14,135	20,680	29,680	35,185	29,970	38,695	45,370	39,185
Net purchases	4,585	4,850	6,975	7,885	9,590	8,500	14,950	10,835	7,545
Activity rate	14.7	19.8	24.7	29.4	32.4	29.8	30.8	27.8	22.9

[a]Includes funds of corporations, unions, and multiemployer groups, and nonprofit organizations; also deferred profit sharing funds.

[b]Mutual funds reporting to Investment Company Institute, a group whose assets constitute about 90 percent of the assets of all open-end investment companies.

[c]Includes both general and separate accounts.

Note: Transactions may not add to totals because figures are rounded to nearest $5 million.

Source: Securities and Exchange Commission, *Stock Transactions of Selected Financial Institutions and Foreigners, 1973*: April 3, 1974, p. 404.

Table 2-2
Assets of Private Noninsured Pension Funds (in Millions of Dollars, End of Year)

	1959	1960	1961	1962	1963	1964	1965	1966	1967	1968	1969	1970	1971	1972	1973
Book value															
Cash and deposits	540	550	660	710	770	890	940	900	1,320	1,590	1,620	1,800	1,640	1,860	2,300
U.S. government securities	2,810	2,680	2,720	2,920	3,050	3,190	2,990	2,750	2,320	2,760	2,790	3,030	2,730	3,690	4,330
Corporate and other bonds	14,080	15,700	16,880	18,100	19,560	21,420	23,130	25,230	26,360	27,000	27,610	29,670	29,010	28,210	29,810
Preferred stock	770	780	760	750	710	650	750	790	980	1,330	1,760	1,740	1,770	1,480	1,240
Common stock	8,670	10,730	13,340	15,730	18,120	20,950	25,120	29,070	34,950	41,740	47,860	51,740	62,780	74,580	79,200
Own company	780	890	1,040	1,180	1,340	1,550	1,830	2,090	2,560	2,800	3,020	3,270	3,520	3,880	n.a.
Other companies	7,890	9,850	12,300	14,540	16,780	19,400	23,290	26,980	32,380	38,940	44,840	48,480	59,260	70,710	n.a.
Mortgages	990	1,300	1,560	1,880	2,220	2,780	3,380	3,910	4,080	4,070	4,220	4,300	3,680	3,000	2,710
Other assets	1,190	1,400	1,590	1,800	2,120	2,540	2,870	3,520	4,230	4,580	4,720	4,730	4,800	4,710	4,770
Total assets	29,050	33,140	37,510	41,890	46,550	52,420	59,180	66,180	74,240	83,070	90,580	97,010	106,420	117,530	124,360
Market value															
Cash and deposits	500	500	700	700	800	900	900	900	1,300	1,600	1,600	1,800	1,600	1,900	2,300
U.S. government securities	2,600	2,700	2,700	2,900	3,000	3,200	2,900	2,700	2,200	2,600	2,600	3,000	2,800	3,700	4,400
Corporate and other bonds	12,500	14,600	15,900	17,500	18,800	20,700	21,900	22,500	22,600	22,400	21,300	24,900	26,100	26,200	27,200
Preferred stock	700	700	700	700	700	700	800	800	1,000	1,400	1,600	1,600	2,000	1,900	1,000
Common stock	13,800	15,800	22,100	21,200	27,000	33,000	40,000	38,700	50,100	60,100	59,800	65,500	86,600	113,400	88,000
Own company	1,800	2,000	3,000	2,600	3,100	4,000	4,400	3,500	5,000	5,700	5,700	5,900	7,500	8,800	n.a.
Other companies	12,100	13,800	19,100	18,600	23,800	29,000	35,600	35,200	45,100	54,400	54,200	59,500	79,100	104,600	n.a.
Mortgages	1,000	1,300	1,600	1,900	2,200	2,800	3,400	3,800	4,000	3,600	3,500	3,600	3,200	2,700	2,400
Other assets	1,200	1,400	1,600	1,800	2,200	2,600	3,000	3,500	4,200	4,300	4,300	4,300	4,500	4,600	4,700
Total assets	32,400	37,100	45,300	46,700	54,600	63,900	72,900	72,800	85,500	96,000	94,600	104,700	126,900	154,300	129,900

n.a. = Not available.

Note: Includes deferred profit sharing funds of corporations, unions, multiemployer groups, and nonprofit organizations. Figures may not add to total because of rounding.

Source: Securities and Exchange Commission, *Private Noninsured Pension Funds, 1973*, April 17, 1974; *Statistical Bulletin*, December 1969, p. 37-38.

Corporate Pension Contributions

In a recent survey of 479 companies conducted by Standard and Poor's/Inter Capital, Inc., it was found that the costs of providing retirement benefits to corporate employees are becoming an increasingly important element in the total expense of doing business.[16] The survey found that the amount of corporate contributions to all types of pension plans relative to total payroll costs increased from an average of 4.7 percent in 1967 to 5.5 percent in 1972 (see Table 2-3). Moreover, the amount of pension contributions relative to total expenses before taxes increased from an average of 1.5 percent in 1967 to 1.7 percent in 1972 (see Table 2-4). Relative to either gross or net corporate income, these ratios would obviously be very much larger. The same trends are revealed throughout the spectrum of all industry categories.

Continuing with this survey, between 1967 and 1971 corporate contributions to company controlled noninsured pension plans increased 50.3 percent, or at a compound annual rate of about 11 percent. This rapid rate reflects the formation of new plans during the period as well as increases in the number of qualified employees and the liberalization of existing plan provisions.

The survey found that pension contributions increased 12.2 percent in 1972, and thus amounted to more than $3.8 billion. These companies estimate that contributions will increase 12.9 percent in 1973 and 11.5 percent in 1974, at which time they will reach nearly $5 billion. See Tables 2-5 and 2-6 for further clarification as to the trends in pension contributions for 1974.

As the aforementioned pension study has demonstrated, employer contributions are becoming a larger and larger percentage of both labor costs and total costs. This fact must always be kept in mind in order to understand fully the corporations' desire to maximize the investment return on their pension portfolios.

According to the Securities and Exchange Commission, employer contributions to noninsured private pension funds increased dramatically in the 1960-73 period. As can easily be seen in Table 2-7, in 1960 employers contributed $3 billion to their pension plans while by 1972 this figure had increased over 400 percent to $12.7 billion.[17] The 1973 figures show that $14 billion was contributed by corporations to their noninsured pension funds.

The increase in pension contributions will probably accelerate in

Table 2-3
Total Company Contributions to All Types of Plans Relative to Total Payrolls (Percent)

Industry	1967			1972		
	Mean	Median	Range	Mean	Median	Range
Primary metals	5.8	6.0	1.6-10.3	6.8	7.5	2.0-11.0
Machinery	3.2	3.3	0.8- 6.3	4.6	4.6	0.0-10.7
Electrical machinery	2.8	2.5	0.0- 7.5	3.9	3.0	1.0-11.0
Transportation equipment	3.6	3.3	0.4- 8.0	4.9	4.9	1.5-12.0
Fabricated metals	2.6	2.5	0.7- 5.6	4.2	4.2	1.7- 5.8
Instruments	3.7	3.5	1.0- 7.2	4.1	4.5	0.7- 5.8
Chemicals	4.9	4.3	0.0-10.9	5.6	4.7	1.8-15.0
Petroleum	5.0	4.7	1.6- 8.7	5.9	5.6	2.5-11.8
Paper	1.1	1.3	0.0- 1.9	5.5	4.3	3.6- 8.5
Rubber & plastics	7.0	5.0	4.0-12.0	7.6	7.0	4.9-11.0
Construction materials	4.6	4.3	1.2- 9.0	4.9	5.3	0.6- 7.0
Textiles & apparel	2.4	1.6	0.0- 5.9	3.4	3.1	0.9- 7.2
Food & beverages	4.7	4.4	1.6- 9.2	5.2	5.2	2.5- 7.0
Miscellaneous manufacturing	3.3	3.5	0.5- 5.4	4.0	3.4	0.8-10.9
Mining	6.8	3.3	1.7-22.7	7.4	4.8	2.8-17.6
Transportation & communications	4.8	4.0	0.5- 9.8	6.5	4.8	0.4-20.4
Electric utilities	6.2	6.3	2.9- 9.3	5.8	5.8	2.3- 9.0
Gas utilities	7.8	7.1	2.8-13.0	8.1	8.1	3.9-12.0
Banks	6.9	6.2	3.4-11.6	5.6	5.3	2.5-11.0
Insurance companies	7.6	5.8	3.0-26.0	6.0	6.0	2.4-15.0
Other commercial	3.7	3.0	1.0-14.0	4.8	3.0	1.3-23.0
All business	4.7	4.0	0.0-26.0	5.5	4.8	0.0-23.0

Source: Standard and Poor's/Inter Capital, Inc., *Third Annual Pension Fund Management Survey*, November 1973.

Table 2-4
Total Company Contributions to All Types of Plans Relative to Total Expenses Before Taxes (Percent)

Industry	1967			1972		
	Mean	Median	Range	Mean	Median	Range
Primary metals	1.9	2.3	0.6- 3.0	2.3	2.0	1.3- 4.0
Machinery	1.5	1.3	0.2- 6.5	2.2	1.9	0.6- 6.4
Electrical machinery	1.6	0.8	0.0- 8.0	1.8	1.1	0.1- 6.7
Transportation equipment	1.3	1.3	0.1- 2.9	1.7	1.7	0.1- 3.8
Fabricated metals	0.9	0.8	0.2- 1.7	1.2	1.1	0.6- 2.2
Instruments	1.3	1.4	0.1- 2.0	1.3	1.3	0.1- 2.1
Chemicals	1.7	1.0	0.0- 6.3	1.8	1.3	0.1- 5.9
Petroleum	0.7	0.6	0.2- 1.7	0.7	0.6	0.3- 1.9
Paper	0.3	0.4	0.0- 0.6	1.4	1.2	0.7- 2.3
Rubber & plastics	1.2	1.2	1.0- 1.4	1.8	1.8	1.5- 2.0
Construction materials	1.4	1.6	0.3- 2.5	1.6	1.8	0.1- 2.4
Textiles & apparel	0.9	0.9	0.0- 1.9	1.1	1.0	0.1- 2.3
Food & beverages	1.3	0.7	0.1- 6.0	1.6	0.8	0.2- 8.0
Miscellaneous manufacturing	0.9	0.8	0.1- 2.4	1.1	0.9	0.6- 2.4
Mining	2.7	1.0	0.3- 9.9	2.3	1.1	0.5- 5.9
Transportation & communications	1.7	1.8	0.2- 5.7	2.5	1.9	0.3-11.0
Electric utilities	1.9	1.9	0.7- 3.8	1.7	1.5	0.6- 5.7
Gas utilities	2.1	2.0	0.5- 4.4	1.7	1.6	0.6- 3.5
Banks	2.0	1.9	1.0- 3.9	1.6	1.1	0.5- 3.6
Insurance companies	3.9	3.6	0.4-13.0	3.3	3.0	0.2- 7.0
Other commercial	1.0	0.5	0.2- 2.0	1.2	0.6	0.3- 4.0
All business	1.5	1.2	0.0-13.0	1.7	1.3	0.1-11.0

Source: Standard and Poor's/Inter Capital, Inc., *Third Annual Pension Fund Management Survey*, November 1973.

Table 2-5
Trends in Company Contributions to Company Controlled Uninsured Pension Funds, by Industry (Millions of Dollars)

Industry	1967	% Change 1967-71	1971	% Change 1971-72	1972	% Change 1972-73	1973	%Change 1973-74	1974
Primary metals	$ 173.2	41.1%	$ 244.4	17.3%	$ 286.7	21.4%	$ 348.1	3.9%	$ 361.7
Machinery	45.7	41.0	64.4	2.6	66.1	7.2	70.9	9.6	77.7
Electrical machinery	299.4	77.4	531.1	19.7	635.7	10.0	699.3	12.3	785.3
Transportation equipment	732.6	50.1	1,099.6	9.7	1,206.3	18.1	1,424.6	13.5	1,616.9
Fabricated metals	50.8	26.9	64.5	10.8	71.5	10.8	79.2	13.0	89.5
Instruments	11.9	45.6	17.3	23.1	21.3	11.5	23.7	25.0	29.6
Chemicals	274.5	18.6	325.6	9.1	355.2	9.9	390.4	9.7	428.3
Petroleum	115.8	58.1	183.1	0.0	183.1	0.0	183.1	4.0	190.4
Paper	8.6	304.5	34.8	11.8	38.9	11.9	43.5	18.9	51.7
Rubber & plastics	44.4	68.3	74.7	7.8	80.5	13.1	91.0	23.8	112.7
Construction materials	40.0	51.3	60.5	22.8	74.3	5.0	78.0	9.7	85.6
Textiles & apparel	10.3	17.5	12.1	12.8	13.6	17.9	16.0	22.1	19.5
Food & beverages	19.7	203.9	59.9	2.2	61.2	0.8	61.7	11.7	68.9
Miscellaneous manufacturing	20.6	107.5	42.7	29.5	55.3	8.1	59.8	10.3	66.0
Mining	9.4	153.4	23.8	4.3	24.8	14.0	28.3	1.8	28.8
Transportation & communications	159.1	53.7	244.5	15.4	282.2	14.4	322.8	11.0	358.3
Electric utilities	83.9	32.0	110.7	17.1	129.6	7.5	139.3	12.1	156.2
Gas utilities	60.8	33.3	81.0	11.6	90.4	8.6	98.2	9.5	107.5
Banks	45.8	25.9	57.7	−2.5	56.3	5.5	59.4	5.6	62.7
Insurance companies	35.9	10.1	39.5	−13.5	34.2	14.4	39.1	15.0	45.0
Other commercial	39.0	48.7	58.0	37.9	80.0	7.8	86.2	13.5	97.8
All Business	2,281.4	50.3	3,429.9	12.2	3,847.2	12.9	4,342.6	11.5	4,840.1

Source: Standard and Poor's/Inter Capital, Inc., *Third Annual Pension Fund Management Survey*, November 1973.

Table 2-6
Trends in Company Contributions to Company Controlled Uninsured Pension Funds, by Size of Fund (Millions of Dollars)

Size of Fund	1967	% Change 1967-71	1971	% Change 1971-72	1972	% Change 1972-73	1973	% Change 1973-74	1974
Under $1 million	$ 0.0	--%	$ 2.7	38.1%	$ 3.7	17.2%	$ 4.3	5.9%	$ 4.6
$1 to $10 million	32.0	51.6	48.5	-7.4	44.9	13.5	51.0	8.9	55.5
$10 to $25 million	50.6	71.2	86.6	-6.1	81.3	14.4	93.0	11.9	104.1
$25 to $50 million	141.0	78.0	251.0	-8.2	230.4	6.7	245.8	8.8	267.4
$50 to $100 million	239.4	56.7	375.1	12.1	420.5	7.5	452.0	8.4	490.0
$100 to $200 million	378.9	42.6	540.3	12.8	609.5	11.5	679.6	10.7	752.3
$200 million and over	1,439.5	47.7	2,125.7	15.6	2,456.9	14.6	2,816.9	12.4	3,166.2
Total	2,281.4	50.3	3,429.9	12.2	3,847.2	12.9	4,342.6	11.5	4,840.1

Source: Standard and Poor's/Inter Capital, Inc., *Third Annual Pension Fund Management Survey*, November 1973.

Table 2-7
Receipts and Disbursements of Private Noninsured Pension Funds (in Millions of Dollars)

	1960[a]	1961[a]	1962	1963	1964	1965	1966	1967	1968	1969	1970	1971	1972	1973
Total receipts	4,709	5,097	6,270	6,780	7,940	9,280	10,330	11,820	13,150	14,150	13,200	17,540	20,070	19,670
Employer contributions	3,016	3,070	3,960	4,170	4,850	5,600	6,360	7,040	7,700	8,490	9,720	11,320	12,740	14,370
Employee contributions	419	438	520	560	600	670	710	790	890	1,010	1,070	1,120	1,200	1,270
Investment income	1,141	1,291	1,580	1,790	2,050	2,390	2,670	2,940	3,190	3,550	3,870	4,100	4,300	4,840
Net profit on sale of assets	101	259	150	230	400	570	520	1,000	1,260	990	(1,590)	900	1,720	(920)
Other receipts	32	39	60	40	40	50	70	60	100	110	130	100	100	110
Total disbursements	1,057	1,202	1,880	2,090	2,420	2,880	3,480	3,990	4,620	5,430	6,180	7,260	8,490	9,540
Benefits paid out	1,027	1,168	1,820	2,020	2,350	2,800	3,380	3,880	4,500	5,290	6,030	7,080	8,300	9,310
Expenses & other disbursements	30	35	70	70	80	90	110	120	120	140	150	180	200	230
Net receipts	3,651	3,895	4,390	4,700	5,510	6,400	6,840	7,830	8,530	8,720	7,020	10,280	11,580	10,130

[a]Does not include pension funds of nonprofit organizations and multiemployer groups.

Note: Includes deferred profit sharing funds and pension funds of corporations, unions, multiemployer groups, and nonprofit organizations. Figures may not add to totals because of rounding.

Source: Securities and Exchange Commission, *Private Noninsured Pension Funds, 1972 and 1973*, September 12, 1973 and 1974.

the years ahead for three major reasons: inflation, more liberalized benefits, and stricter funding and vesting provisions.

In a recent *Harvard Business Review* article, it was pointed out that our present-day private pension system works quite well under low levels of inflation, as evidenced during most of the 1960s.[18] However, if inflation continues at 5 to 10 percent a year, pension plans that link retirement benefits to workers' final pay level (which is the common procedure) will have to find investments yielding 10 to 13 percent annually. Alternatively, they could increase employer contributions to the fund. All this is caused by inflation-induced increased pension benefits that increase costs. Increased contributions will probably be the major effect of inflation, since secure investments at a return of 10 to 13 percent are difficult to find, especially when a trustee must comply with the prudent man rule. If the inflation rate should continue in excess of 10 percent, as we are now experiencing, then contributions must rise astronomically.[19] The fact that the steel industry, among others, has signed inflation escalator clauses as part of its pension agreements increases the likelihood that inflation will significantly magnify pension costs.[20]

The second factor that increases pension costs to the corporations is that of more liberalized benefits. This liberalization has been growing for many years. For example, in 1974 the steel industry signed a labor contract with substantially increased benefits:[21]

1. Retirement age lowered from 65 to 62
2. Retiree guaranteed 85 percent of final pay (including social security)
3. Previously retired workers gained increased benefits
4. Cost of living clause was included.

It has been estimated by a major Wall Street firm that the steel industry's pension costs could rise to $1.1 billion in 1976, that is, a rise of over 87 percent for the life of the contract.[22] Similar liberalized benefits and subsequent increased costs are common in other industries. Pensions have become one of labor's main bargaining points and it most certainly seems that this trend will continue.

On Labor Day, 1974, President Ford signed the much-heralded 247-page Pension Reform Act.[23] With it came significant changes that will dramatically alter employer contributions to the private pension system.

This act mandated that all pension plans must have vesting provisions, that is, employees are to be given unalienable rights to pension benefits after a specified number of years, with the provision that the pension must be fully vested after the employee has worked 15 years at the latest. Moreover, vested benefits must be calculated on early retirement rather than on normal retirement. It is obvious that this new vesting provision alone will substantially increase pension costs.[24]

Pensions also must be fully funded–all vested liabilities must be covered by pension fund assets. Today, about one third of all pensions are not fully funded, thus increasing future pension costs and creating a significant pension liability.[25] It is estimated that there is between $30 and $50 billion of unfunded pension liability due to the provisions of the new law.[26] In fact one company, Bethlehem Steel, has an estimated $1 billion of unfunded pension debt that must come out of earnings and, obviously, will significantly increase pension costs while reducing corporate profits.[27]

Other provisions of this act that will further increase costs include:

1. Using market value instead of book value for actuarial assumptions–significant in today's depressed stock market
2. Contributions to the new government Pension Benefits Guaranty Corporation for pension insurance
3. Increased administrative and disclosure requirements

It is estimated by some analysts that this law alone will cause pension costs to rise by 10 to 15 percent per year, or $2 to $3 billion before taxes.[28]

The corporations are trying their best to offset some of these increased costs with better investment performance. For, as was stated earlier, a minor increase in investment performance could significantly decrease corporate pension contributions. This is the major reason why pensions are so performance conscious today.

Actuarial Assumptions

In an attempt to offset some of the additional costs of pensions, many firms have turned to increasing their actuarial assumptions. This means that they are increasing their hoped-for rate of return. In a recent survey, more than 1,000 firms adjusted upward their assumed rate of return, presumably in order to cut contributions.[29] Interestingly enough, an actuary can be given an identical set of figures for work force and salary increases, and yet produce figures recommending either a 50 percent cut or a doubling of contributions to a pension fund. This can be done merely by raising actuarial assumptions for two or three successive years. A corporation can show earnings increases of from 4 to 8 percent just by increasing the actuarial assumption.[30]

In a study conducted by Standard and Poor's/Inter Capital, Inc., an unmistakable steady uptrend in actuarial assumptions can be seen starting in 1965, when the mean assumption was 3.9 percent. The mean assumption reported for 1971 was 4.7 percent; for 1972 it was 5.0 percent; and for 1973 the figure was 5.1 percent.[31] As can be seen from Tables 2-8 and 2-9, there seems to be no significant difference between industries in their actuarial assumptions. However, there seems to be a clear trend when corporate size is taken into consideration. The largest-sized funds ($200 million and over) generally have the highest mean assumptions. In 1973 this was 5.6 percent. Moreover, it seems quite unsound that some firms have assumptions as high as 10 to 12 percent. It is highly unlikely that such a return will be achieved, thus making contribution costs decrease but having the pension significantly underfunded.

It must be kept in mind that, generally, actuarial assumptions should be lower than actual rates of return. It is necessary to have at least a 3 percent cushion to adjust for a 2 to 3 percent annual rise in labor costs.[32] With today's inflation, such a minimal cushion seems far too small. In spite of this fact, assumptions of 8 to 12 percent are becoming more common.

In light of these very optimistic actuarial projections, many pensions have emphasized equity investments to improve performance during the last decade.

In order to understand better the rationale behind the shift toward greater equity investing, one must look at the performance of common stocks over an extended period. This is especially important for pension funds, which claim to be long-term investors.

NYSE-listed Stock Rates of Return

Professors Lawrence Fisher and J.H. Lorie of The University of Chicago recently conducted a study in which they tested to find the average rate of return for all New York Stock Exchange (NYSE)-

Table 2-8
Actuarial Assumptions for Uninsured Funds: Mean, Median, and Range, 1972 and 1973, by Industry (Percent)

	1972			1973		
Industry	Mean	Median	Range	Mean	Median	Range
Primary metals	5.0	5.0	3.0- 6.5	5.3	5.0	4.5- 6.5
Machinery	5.0	4.7	4.0- 8.0	5.0	4.7	4.0- 8.0
Electrical machinery	5.1	5.0	4.0- 6.0	5.0	5.0	4.0- 6.0
Transportation equipment	5.3	5.0	4.0- 6.0	5.3	5.0	4.0- 6.2
Fabricated metals	5.2	5.0	3.5- 7.0	5.4	5.0	3.5- 8.0
Instruments	4.9	4.9	4.0- 6.5	4.9	4.9	4.0- 6.5
Chemicals	5.5	5.0	4.5-12.0	5.5	5.0	4.5-12.0
Petroleum	5.3	5.0	4.5- 6.0	5.2	5.0	4.5- 6.0
Paper	5.0	5.0	4.0- 7.5	5.2	5.0	4.5- 7.5
Rubber and plastics	5.2	5.0	5.0- 5.5	5.5	5.5	5.0- 6.0
Construction materials	5.1	5.0	4.0- 6.0	5.1	5.2	4.0- 6.0
Textiles and apparel	4.5	4.5	3.5- 5.5	4.7	4.5	3.5- 6.0
Food and beverages	4.8	5.0	4.0- 6.0	4.9	5.0	4.0- 6.0
Miscellaneous manufacturing	4.7	4.5	4.0- 7.0	4.8	4.5	4.0- 7.0
Mining	5.0	5.0	3.5- 7.0	5.1	5.0	3.5- 7.0
Transportation and communications	5.1	5.0	3.5-10.0	5.2	5.0	1.5-10.0
Electric utilities	4.6	4.5	3.5- 6.5	4.7	4.5	3.8- 6.5
Gas utilities	4.9	4.8	4.0- 8.0	5.0	5.0	4.0- 8.0
Banks	5.2	5.5	4.0- 6.0	5.4	5.6	4.0- 6.0
Insurance companies	3.8	4.0	2.3- 5.0	4.1	4.5	2.5- 5.0
Other commercial	4.7	4.5	3.5- 7.5	4.8	4.5	3.5- 7.5
All Business	5.0	5.0	2.3-12.0	5.1	5.0	1.5-12.0

Source: Standard and Poor's/Inter Capital, Inc., *Third Annual Pension Fund Management Survey*, November 1973.

Table 2-9
Actuarial Assumptions for Uninsured Funds: Mean, Median, and Range, 1972 and 1973, by Size of Fund (Percent)

	1972			1973		
Size of Fund	Mean	Median	Range	Mean	Median	Range
Under $1 million	4.9	4.5	3.5- 8.0	4.9	4.5	3.5- 8.0
$1 to $10 million	5.0	4.8	3.5- 8.0	5.1	5.0	3.5- 8.0
$10 to $25 million	4.8	5.0	4.0- 7.0	4.8	5.0	1.5- 8.0
$25 to $50 million	4.9	4.8	2.3-12.0	5.2	5.0	4.0-12.0
$50 to $100 million	4.8	4.8	3.8- 6.0	5.0	5.0	3.9- 6.0
$100 to $200 million	5.1	5.0	2.5- 7.5	5.2	5.0	2.5- 7.5
$200 million and over	5.5	5.5	3.5-10.0	5.6	5.5	4.5-10.0
Total	5.0	5.0	2.3-12.0	5.1	5.0	1.5-12.0

Source: Standard and Poor's/Inter Capital, Inc., *Third Annual Pension Fund Management Survey*, November 1973.

listed common stocks during the 1926-65 period.[33] They employed average annual rates compounded annually, and assumed equal initial investments in each listed common stock. These rates take into consideration dividends, commissions, and other pertinent factors affecting the actual rates of return.

The findings of this study were quite extensive but only a few of the major revelations are discussed here. Over the entire period, 1926-65, the average annual rate of return compounded annually (assuming reinvestment of dividends and that the investor was tax-exempt—e.g., pensions) was 9.3 percent (see Table 2-10). Without dividend reinvestment the return for that period would be 7.3 percent (see Table 2-11). Intraperiod returns varied significantly. For example, assuming dividend reinvestment, the mean return was 12.6 percent for the 1945-65 period. During the prewar period from December 1929 to December 1941 the mean equity return was negative 0.6 percent. These years before World War II were the longest periods with negative returns.

Since most institutional investors look at the postwar years as being highly indicative of future trends, the following statistics clarify the reasons for the significant shift to equity investing by these institutions. The mean annual return for the 1941-65 period was 17.5 percent, while for the 1945-65 period, positive returns were earned for 95 percent of the 210 overlapping periods. Also, there was

Table 2-10

Rates of Return on Investment in Common Stocks Listed on the New York Stock Exchange with Reinvestment of Dividends (Percent per Annum Compounded Annually)

To	From 1/26	12/26	12/27	12/28	12/29	12/30	12/31	12/32	12/33	12/34	12/35	12/36	12/37	12/38	12/39	12/40	12/41	12/42	12/43	12/44
12/26	−1.6																			
12/27	15.3	30.0																		
12/28	23.9	37.7	45.5																	
12/29	7.8	9.6	0.1	−30.0																
12/30	−2.3	−3.5	−13.0	−31.7	−37.2															
12/31	−11.1	−13.5	−21.7	−36.3	−40.8	−47.8														
12/32	−11.0	−12.7	−19.0	−30.3	−32.1	−31.0	−11.1													
12/33	−2.7	−3.2	−7.7	−15.6	−11.8	−1.3	36.9	108.4												
12/34	−1.2	−1.6	−5.2	−11.3	−7.0	2.4	28.2	55.0	13.8											
12/35	2.2	2.1	−0.8	−5.7	−0.5	9.3	32.9	53.5	31.2	50.4										
12/36	6.6	5.5	3.1	−0.4	5.3	15.3	37.5	54.5	40.9	56.8	63.9									
12/37	0.5	0.1	−2.3	−6.2	−2.8	3.3	16.1	23.1	8.2	6.6	−10.9	−46.0								
12/38	2.8	2.5	0.4	−2.9	0.9	7.0	18.7	25.1	12.9	12.4	1.1	−16.2	30.7							
12/39	2.6	2.3	0.3	−2.6	0.9	6.0	15.7	20.5	10.1	9.0	0.4	−11.2	12.9	−3.3						
12/40	1.9	1.6	−0.2	−3.0	0.2	4.7	13.0	16.9	7.9	6.4	−1.1	−9.8	6.3	−5.0	−9.9					
12/41	1.2	0.9	−0.8	−3.3	−0.5	3.5	10.8	13.8	5.8	4.2	−1.9	−9.2	2.6	−5.5	−9.0	−10.2				
12/42	2.0	1.9	0.4	−1.9	0.9	4.8	11.6	14.3	7.2	6.0	0.9	−4.9	6.1	0.6	1.1	7.6	31.1			
12/43	3.5	3.6	2.2	0.2	3.1	7.2	13.8	16.5	10.2	9.7	5.5	0.9	12.3	9.4	12.1	22.2	47.1	56.7		
12/44	4.6	4.7	3.5	1.7	4.7	8.7	15.2	17.9	12.3	12.0	8.4	4.6	15.7	13.7	17.1	26.8	45.6	49.3	38.1	
12/45	6.3	6.5	5.5	3.9	7.0	11.3	17.6	20.4	15.4	15.5	12.4	9.3	20.3	19.4	23.7	33.6	51.4	55.4	50.1	59.8

12/46	5.5	5.7	4.7	3.2	6.0	9.9	15.6	18.0	13.3	13.1	10.2	7.2	16.3	15.0	17.8	24.2	34.8	34.5	26.0	20.2
12/47	5.3	5.6	4.6	3.1	5.8	9.3	14.6	16.8	12.4	12.1	9.4	6.7	14.7	13.6	15.5	20.3	27.5	26.3	18.9	13.2
12/48	5.1	5.2	4.2	2.8	5.2	8.5	13.5	15.5	11.3	11.0	8.4	5.8	12.7	11.7	13.3	17.0	22.5	20.8	14.2	9.1
12/49	5.7	5.8	4.9	3.6	6.0	9.1	13.8	15.7	11.7	11.5	9.1	6.8	13.3	12.3	13.9	17.3	22.2	20.8	15.2	11.4
12/50	6.5	6.7	5.9	4.6	7.0	10.2	14.9	16.7	12.9	12.8	10.6	8.5	14.8	14.1	15.6	19.0	23.5	22.4	17.9	15.0
12/51	6.9	7.1	6.4	5.1	7.5	10.6	15.1	16.7	13.1	13.1	11.0	9.0	14.8	14.1	15.6	18.6	22.6	21.6	17.7	15.2
12/52	7.0	7.2	6.5	5.3	7.6	10.5	14.8	16.4	13.0	13.0	11.0	9.0	14.5	13.8	15.1	17.9	21.5	20.4	16.8	14.5
12/53	6.6	6.8	6.1	5.0	7.1	9.8	13.9	15.3	12.2	12.1	10.2	8.3	13.3	12.5	13.7	16.1	19.3	18.1	14.8	12.5
12/54	6.1	8.2	7.6	6.4	8.7	11.4	15.5	17.0	14.0	14.1	12.2	10.5	15.5	14.8	16.2	18.7	21.9	21.0	18.2	16.4
12/55	8.4	8.6	8.0	6.9	9.2	11.9	15.9	17.4	14.5	14.6	12.7	11.1	15.9	15.2	16.6	18.8	21.8	21.1	18.6	16.9
12/56	8.5	8.7	8.1	7.0	9.2	11.8	15.7	17.1	14.4	14.4	12.6	11.1	15.6	15.1	16.2	18.2	20.8	20.2	17.9	16.4
12/57	7.8	7.9	7.3	6.3	8.3	10.7	14.3	15.5	12.9	12.9	11.2	9.7	13.9	13.2	14.2	15.9	18.3	17.5	15.1	13.6
12/58	8.8	9.0	8.4	7.5	9.5	11.9	15.5	16.7	14.3	14.4	12.7	11.3	15.5	15.0	16.0	17.8	20.2	19.4	17.3	16.0
12/59	8.9	9.1	8.5	7.6	9.7	12.1	15.6	16.8	14.4	14.5	12.8	11.5	15.6	15.0	16.0	17.6	19.9	19.1	17.1	15.8
12/60	8.8	9.0	8.3	7.5	9.4	11.6	14.9	16.1	13.9	13.9	12.3	11.1	14.8	14.2	15.1	16.6	18.7	17.9	15.9	14.6
12/61	9.3	9.5	8.9	8.1	9.9	12.2	15.4	16.6	14.4	14.5	13.0	11.8	15.4	15.0	15.8	17.3	19.3	18.5	16.5	15.4
12/62	8.6	8.8	8.2	7.3	9.1	11.2	14.3	15.3	13.2	13.3	11.8	10.7	14.0	13.5	14.3	15.6	17.3	16.5	14.6	13.5
12/63	8.9	9.1	8.5	7.7	9.5	11.6	14.6	15.6	13.5	13.6	12.2	11.0	14.3	13.8	14.6	15.8	17.4	16.7	14.9	13.9
12/64	9.1	9.3	8.8	7.9	9.6	11.6	14.5	15.6	13.6	13.7	12.4	11.3	14.4	14.0	14.7	15.8	17.4	16.7	15.0	14.0
12/65	9.3	9.5	9.0	8.2	10.0	12.0	14.9	15.9	13.9	14.0	12.6	11.6	14.6	14.2	14.9	16.0	17.5	16.9	15.4	14.4

Table 2-10 (cont.)

To	From 12/45	12/46	12/47	12/48	12/49	12/50	12/51	12/52	12/53	12/54	12/55	12/56	12/57	12/58	12/59	12/60	12/61	12/21	12/63	12/64
12/46	-9.9																			
12/47	-4.4	-0.5																		
12/48	-3.5	-1.0	-2.9																	
12/49	1.9	5.4	8.2	19.3																
12/50	7.8	12.4	16.6	27.0	35.8															
12/51	9.4	13.3	16.4	23.1	25.2	14.9														
12/52	9.4	12.9	15.2	19.7	19.8	12.4	8.9													
12/53	7.9	10.5	12.1	15.0	13.7	7.5	3.5	-3.1												
12/54	12.5	15.5	17.7	21.3	21.6	17.9	18.5	22.8	54.8											
12/55	13.4	16.2	18.2	21.4	21.7	18.5	19.1	22.2	37.2	19.0										
12/56	13.3	15.6	17.2	19.8	20.0	17.0	16.9	18.6	26.7	13.3	6.5									
12/57	10.5	12.3	13.5	15.3	14.8	12.0	11.1	11.1	14.5	3.4	-3.7	-12.9								
12/58	13.2	15.2	16.7	18.7	18.6	16.5	16.5	17.5	21.9	14.5	13.0	17.4	57.9							
12/59	13.3	15.3	16.6	18.6	18.6	16.6	16.6	17.6	21.2	15.0	14.0	17.6	36.0	14.4						
12/60	12.2	14.0	15.2	16.8	16.5	14.9	14.8	15.3	17.8	12.4	11.2	13.1	21.9	6.4	-1.9					
12/61	13.2	14.9	16.0	17.5	17.3	16.0	16.0	16.6	19.0	14.6	13.9	16.1	23.7	13.6	12.9	27.6				
12/62	11.3	12.8	13.7	14.9	14.5	13.1	12.8	13.0	14.7	10.5	9.4	10.4	15.1	6.3	3.8	5.9	-13.3			
12/63	11.8	13.2	14.0	15.2	14.9	13.5	13.3	13.5	15.0	11.3	10.4	11.5	15.7	8.7	7.4	10.4	2.0	17.7		
12/64	12.1	13.4	14.2	15.3	15.0	13.7	13.5	13.8	15.3	11.9	11.2	12.3	16.2	10.4	9.7	12.8	7.6	18.5	16.3	
12/65	12.6	14.1	14.9	15.9	15.8	14.5	14.3	14.7	16.2	13.1	12.5	13.6	17.7	12.7	12.4	15.9	12.9	22.6	23.4	28.3

Note: Cash-to-portfolio, tax-exempt.

Source: Lawrence Fisher and James Lorie, "Rates of Return on Investments in Common Stocks: Year-by-Year Record," *Journal of Business*, July 1968, p. 296.

no interval of more than 4 years in which returns were less than 7 percent. In fact, in the postwar years there was no 10-year period during which the return was less than a healthy 11 percent per annum.

The above findings convey the impression that if one just held on to equity and disregarded minor downturns, equity investing would be quite profitable. This would seem especially so in comparison to bond returns, which were in the 4 to 5 percent range during this period.

Thus, the return of 12.6 percent during the 1945-65 period provides a partial justification for increased institutional equity investing. More importantly, this explains the extreme optimism on the part of pensions, reflected by their actuarial assumptions and expected rates of return. The 9.3 percent return for the 1926-65 period is considered quite respectable. Surprisingly, the negative return for the 1927-41 period is taken as a unique situation not likely to recur.

In a recent update to the Fisher and Lorie study, a financial service analyzed the returns of equal investments in all stocks traded on the New York Stock Exchange.[34] This analysis examined the average annual returns on investment for a tax-exempt (e.g., pensions) investor.[35]

The study found that, for the most recent 10-year period from 1964 to 1973, the mean annual return on NYSE-listed common stocks was a paltry 2.3 percent, compared with the 1959-68 and 1949-58 decades of 16.6 percent and 18.2 percent, respectively. As can be seen in Table 2-12, during the most recent five-year period from 1969 to 1973 the mean annual return was a dismal –6 percent. Only three other five-year periods were worse than the 1969-73 period, and these were all prewar periods.[36] In fact, by historical standards, the last five years have been among the worst in modern stock market history. It is strongly hoped, naturally, that this recent downturn will be followed by a significant bull market. Historically, this has been the pattern. For example, the mean annual return for the 1932-36 period was 42.3 percent.

The study, nevertheless, ends on a positive note, pointing out that since 1926 the mean 10-year NYSE-listed stock performance was 13.4 percent, while for high grade bonds it was a significantly lower 3.0 percent. In recognition of this sharp comparison, the study concludes that common stocks are a good long-term investment

Table 2-11
Rates of Return on Investment in Common Stocks Listed on the New York Stock Exchange without Reinvestment of Dividends (Percent per Annum Compounded Annually)

To	From 1/26	12/26	12/27	12/28	12/29	12/30	12/31	12/32	12/33	12/34	12/35	12/36	12/37	12/38	12/39	12/40	12/41	12/42	12/43	12/44
12/26	−1.8																			
12/27	14.9	29.9																		
12/28	23.3	37.5	45.6																	
12/29	8.0	10.1	0.6	−30.0																
12/30	−1.2	−2.3	−12.1	−31.5	−36.9															
12/31	−8.9	−11.3	−20.1	−35.8	−40.5	−47.6														
12/32	−9.1	−11.0	−18.1	−30.5	−32.4	−31.4	−11.5													
12/33	−2.5	−3.0	−8.0	−16.9	−13.1	−2.4	36.3	108.8												
12/34	−1.4	−1.8	−5.9	−12.9	−8.4	1.3	27.9	55.5	13.7											
12/35	1.5	1.5	−1.8	−7.5	−2.1	8.3	32.7	54.0	31.1	50.4										
12/36	6.3	4.9	2.2	−1.9	4.0	14.5	37.5	55.3	41.1	57.2	64.2									
12/37	0.4	0.0	−2.9	−7.5	−3.7	3.2	17.4	25.5	9.5	8.0	−9.9	−45.9								
12/38	2.1	1.9	−0.6	−4.7	−0.5	6.4	19.5	27.0	13.6	13.2	1.2	−16.9	30.5							
12/39	1.9	1.7	−0.7	−4.4	−0.5	5.5	16.6	22.5	10.8	9.7	0.3	−12.2	12.8	−3.6						
12/40	1.5	1.2	−1.1	−4.6	−1.0	4.2	14.2	19.3	8.6	7.0	−1.2	−10.7	6.3	−5.3	−10.1					
12/41	1.0	0.7	−1.4	−4.7	−1.5	3.4	12.4	16.6	6.8	5.1	−2.0	−10.1	2.8	−5.7	−9.1	−10.1				
12/42	1.5	1.4	−0.6	−3.7	−0.5	4.3	12.8	16.7	7.8	6.4	0.4	−6.2	5.9	−0.0	0.4	7.1	31.1			
12/43	2.6	2.6	0.9	−1.9	1.4	6.2	14.5	18.3	10.3	9.6	4.6	−0.8	11.7	8.4	11.2	21.8	47.7	57.8		
12/44	3.4	3.5	1.9	−0.6	2.8	7.6	15.5	19.3	12.0	11.6	7.2	2.7	14.8	12.5	16.0	26.3	46.3	50.2	38.2	
12/45	4.7	5.0	3.6	1.3	4.8	9.7	17.4	21.2	14.6	14.6	10.9	7.1	19.1	17.8	22.3	32.9	52.0	56.1	50.1	59.8

12/46	4.2	4.4	3.0	0.9	4.1	8.6	15.8	19.4	12.9	12.7	9.1	5.4	15.7	14.1	17.1	24.2	36.1	35.9	26.7	20.9
12/47	4.2	4.4	3.0	0.9	4.0	8.2	15.2	18.5	12.2	11.9	8.5	5.1	14.4	13.0	15.2	20.7	29.2	28.1	19.8	13.8
12/48	4.1	4.2	2.8	0.8	3.7	7.8	14.5	17.6	11.5	11.1	7.7	4.4	12.9	11.5	13.4	18.0	24.8	23.1	15.5	10.0
12/49	4.5	4.6	3.3	1.4	4.2	8.1	14.6	17.6	11.8	11.4	8.2	5.2	13.3	12.0	13.8	18.1	24.4	22.8	16.1	11.8
12/50	5.1	5.2	4.0	2.2	5.0	8.9	15.3	18.2	12.5	12.3	9.4	6.6	14.3	13.3	15.1	19.4	25.2	23.9	18.3	14.8
12/51	5.4	5.5	4.4	2.7	5.4	9.2	15.4	18.1	12.7	12.6	9.8	7.0	14.4	13.3	15.1	19.0	24.4	23.1	18.1	15.1
12/52	5.5	5.6	4.6	2.9	5.5	9.2	15.2	17.9	12.7	12.5	9.8	7.2	14.2	13.1	14.9	18.5	23.5	22.2	17.4	14.5
12/53	5.3	5.4	4.4	2.7	5.3	8.8	14.7	17.4	12.2	12.0	9.3	6.8	13.4	12.3	13.9	17.3	21.9	20.4	15.8	13.0
12/54	6.1	6.3	5.3	3.8	6.3	9.8	15.5	18.1	13.2	13.2	10.6	8.3	14.8	13.8	15.5	18.9	23.4	22.3	18.2	15.9
12/55	6.4	6.6	5.7	4.2	6.7	10.1	15.8	18.3	13.5	13.5	11.0	8.8	15.1	14.1	15.8	19.0	23.3	22.2	18.5	16.3
12/56	6.5	6.7	5.8	4.3	6.8	10.1	15.6	18.1	13.5	13.4	11.0	8.8	14.9	14.1	15.5	18.5	22.5	21.5	18.0	15.9
12/57	6.1	6.3	5.4	3.9	6.3	9.5	15.0	17.4	12.7	12.6	10.2	8.0	13.9	12.9	14.3	17.1	20.9	19.8	16.1	13.9
12/58	6.8	7.0	6.1	4.7	7.1	10.3	15.6	17.9	13.5	13.5	11.1	9.2	14.9	14.1	15.4	18.2	22.0	20.9	17.5	15.6
12/59	6.9	7.1	6.2	4.9	7.2	10.4	15.6	17.9	13.5	13.5	11.2	9.3	14.9	14.1	15.4	18.1	21.7	20.7	17.3	15.5
12/60	6.8	7.0	6.1	4.8	6.1	10.1	15.3	17.6	13.3	13.2	11.0	9.1	14.4	13.6	14.9	17.4	21.0	19.9	16.5	14.7
12/61	7.2	7.4	6.5	5.2	7.5	10.5	15.5	17.8	13.5	13.6	11.4	9.6	14.8	14.0	15.3	17.8	21.2	20.1	16.9	15.2
12/62	6.8	7.0	6.1	4.8	7.0	10.0	15.0	17.3	12.9	12.9	10.7	8.9	14.0	13.2	14.4	16.8	20.2	19.0	15.7	13.9
12/63	7.0	7.2	6.3	5.1	7.3	10.2	15.1	17.4	13.1	13.1	10.9	9.1	14.2	13.4	14.6	16.9	20.1	19.0	15.8	14.1
12/64	7.1	7.3	6.5	5.3	7.4	10.2	15.1	17.3	13.1	13.1	11.0	9.3	14.2	13.4	14.6	16.9	20.1	19.0	15.9	14.3
12/65	7.3	7.5	6.7	5.5	7.7	10.5	15.3	17.4	13.3	13.3	11.2	9.6	14.4	13.6	14.8	17.0	20.1	19.0	16.1	14.5

Table 2-11 (cont.)

To	From 12/45	12/46	12/47	12/48	12/49	12/50	12/51	12/52	12/53	12/54	12/55	12/56	12/57	12/58	12/59	12/60	12/61	12/62	12/63	12/64
12/46	−9.8																			
12/47	−4.6	−0.7																		
12/48	−3.6	−1.0	−2.8																	
12/49	1.2	4.9	7.7	18.9																
12/50	6.6	11.4	15.7	26.5	35.7															
12/51	8.1	12.4	15.8	23.1	25.6	15.0														
12/52	8.3	12.1	14.8	20.0	20.3	12.5	8.8													
12/53	7.2	10.2	12.2	15.8	14.6	7.9	3.6	−3.2												
12/54	10.9	14.4	16.9	21.1	21.5	17.3	17.8	22.1	54.8											
12/55	11.8	15.0	17.4	21.2	21.6	18.0	18.5	21.8	37.7	19.0										
12/56	11.7	14.6	16.5	19.8	20.1	16.6	16.6	18.5	27.4	13.5	6.6									
12/57	9.8	12.2	13.7	16.3	15.7	12.4	11.6	11.8	15.9	4.0	−3.3	−12.7								
12/58	11.9	14.4	16.2	18.9	18.8	16.2	16.2	17.4	22.5	14.3	12.6	16.9	58.1							
12/59	12.0	14.4	16.2	18.8	18.8	16.3	16.4	17.5	21.8	14.9	13.7	17.3	36.5	14.6						
12/60	11.3	13.6	15.2	17.4	17.2	15.0	14.9	15.6	18.7	12.5	11.1	13.1	22.6	6.6	−2.1					
12/61	12.0	14.2	15.8	17.9	17.7	15.8	15.8	16.6	19.7	14.4	13.6	15.9	24.2	13.5	12.7	27.9				
12/62	10.7	12.7	14.0	15.8	15.5	13.4	13.1	13.5	15.8	10.7	9.4	10.6	15.9	6.5	3.8	6.1	−13.5			
12/63	11.0	13.0	14.3	16.0	15.7	13.7	13.5	13.8	16.0	11.4	10.4	11.6	16.5	8.8	7.2	10.6	1.8	18.0		
12/64	11.3	13.2	14.4	16.1	15.8	13.9	13.7	14.1	16.2	11.9	11.0	12.3	16.7	10.3	9.4	12.8	7.3	18.6	16.4	
12/65	11.7	13.7	14.9	16.5	16.3	14.5	14.3	14.8	16.9	13.0	12.2	13.5	18.1	12.4	12.1	15.8	12.5	22.7	23.4	28.3

Note: Cash-to-portfolio, tax-exempt.

Source: Lawrence Fisher and James Lorie "Rates of Return on Investments In Common Stocks: Year-by-Year Record 1926-1965," *Journal of Business*, July 1968, p. 296.

Table 2-12
The Average Annual Compounded Rate of Return of Common Stocks for Selected Periods[a]

Bear Markets–Five-year Periods		Bull Markets–Five-year Periods		Ten-year Periods	
Period	Mean Annual Return	Period	Mean Annual Return	Period	Mean Annual Return
1927-31	–35.7%	1932-36	42.3%	1929-38	9.2%
1928-32	–25.8	1941-45	42.2	1939-48	11.1
1937-41	–7.3	1931-35	30.7	1949-58	18.2
1969-73	–6.0	1942-46	30.0	1959-68	16.6
1959-63	+8.0	1964-68	21.8	1964-73	2.3

Investment Medium	Mean 10-year Return[b]	Range of 10-year Returns
All NYSE-listed stocks	13.4%	2.3% to 21.8%
Triple A bonds	3.0	–0.9 to 7.6
Savings and loan account	3.4	2.5 to 5.0

[a]Assumes no taxes and a transaction charge of 1 percent.

[b]The average for each 10-year period beginning each year since 1927.

Source: "Market Place," *New York Times*, July 18, 1974. © 1974 by The New York Times Company. Reprinted by permission.

notwithstanding short-term vacillations. These short-term declines are eclipsed by long-term capital appreciation. Hopefully, history will repeat itself.

A recent study by a major investment banking firm analyzed the relative total performance of different financial instruments for the five-year period 1969-73. This is of particular interest since the Fisher and Lorie study demonstrated most emphatically that, excluding the depression years, common stocks out-performed bonds and other debt instruments. Partly because of this thinking, significant flows of private and public pension funds have been shifted from bonds to stocks in the last 15 years.

As can be seen in Table 2-13, total performance consists of price change plus dividends or interest payments as a percent of starting values. Performance for common stocks was a negative 15 percent for the year 1973.[37] In the same year all other financial instruments analyzed had positive returns, with three-month certificates of deposit providing the highest return at 8 percent. In fact, for the entire five-year period, the average annual rate of return was 7 percent for three-month certificates of deposit, with bonds not far behind and common stocks in last place at 3 percent. Furthermore, if Table 2-13 were extended to incorporate the first half of 1974,

Table 2-13
Total Performance of Selected Market Sectors 1969-73[a]

	U.S. Governments		High-grade Corporates	Prime Municipals	Common	Three-month Certificates of
	Long	Medium	Long	Long	Stock[b]	Deposit
1969	−5%	−1%	−8%	−17%	−8%	+8%
1970	+12	+16	+18	+21	+4	+8
1971	+13	+9	+11	+13	+14	+5
1972	+6	+4	+7	+4	+19	+5
1973	0	+4	+1	+4	−15	+8
1969-73 annual average	+5	+6	+6	+5	+3	+7

Note: Excludes reinvestment.

[a]Total performance equals price change + dividend income as percent of starting value.

[b]Based on Standard and Poor's 500 Stock Index.

Source: Salomon Brothers, *1973 Annual Review of the Bond Market*, New York, 1974, p. 4.

common stock return would be a negative 11.84 percent while three-month certificates would be in the 10-11 percent range.[38]

Upon closer scrutiny of this table, it becomes quite apparent that only during two of the previous five years were common stocks the leading performers. Moreover, during the 1969-73 period, the three-month certificates of deposit were far superior to all types of investments for consistency of return and reduced volatility. This relationship has also been consistent during the first six months of 1974.

Although common stocks were the highest performers in the postwar period, this trend did not recur during the most recent five-year period. Unfortunately, many institutions shifted their portfolio mix towards far greater common stocks at a time when other investment vehicles with less risk would have been more rewarding.

3 Performance Studies

Pension Funds

Competition for the all-important pension dollar has been quite active for the last several years. In fact, this keen rivalry will most likely accelerate in the years ahead.

One very indicative sign of this competition was reflected in a recent advertisement in the *Institutional Investor.* This question was posed in bold print:[1] "An annual 8% return? On a pension and profit sharing fund? Over the last 10 years?"[2] The advertisement then went on to answer its own question with a positive "YES!," stating further that its bank placed in the top 1 percent of the 299 professionally managed retirement funds monitored by A.G. Becker and Co. from 1967 to 1973.[3]

The bank does not stop here but continues on to show its potential client that $10 million invested in the fund during this period would have generated approximately $3,860,000 more than the same investment in (A.G.) Becker's median fund.[4] In order to make its point still clearer, it shows that the Standard and Poor's (S&P's) 500 Stock Index had a 6 percent compounded return for the period and only 15 percent of all money managers did better than the S & P 500. But then the clincher is thrown: "Our Fund's return: 8%. Yours?"[5]

In order to protect itself, the bank goes on to state that past performance is no guarantee for future performance, but they seem to imply that it certainly helps.

This type of marketing is quite indicative of the frantic competition in the field. This form of advertising is becoming quite common and is, in fact, becoming bolder all the time. One such recent ad opened with the statement, "It pays to think about firing a pension fund manager. . . ."[6]

Two important reasons for this acceleration in competition are the 1974 pension bill, which will be much more costly, and the heavy pension fund losses over the last two years. Both factors will spark pensions to increase their search for the best investment manager.

Performance, of course, is of paramount importance to the pension trustee. However, it is also imperative to know performance for an efficient allocation of financial resources. If the allocation was at a suboptimum level, it was thus partially misallocated.

In discussing institutional investors, Irwin Friend asserts that:

> Their contribution to economic efficiency depends to a great extent on their ability to help the equity markets transfer capital into the most profitable investments in productive goods (with due allowances for differences in risk).[7]

It is necessary to have an understanding of capital market and portfolio theory in order to comprehend recent performance studies of the institutional investor.

Methodology[8]

Risk-adjusted return was used quite extensively in many recent studies of institutional investment performance.[9] Portfolio theory and its application are discussed to obtain a clearer picture of performance results.

The methodology employed in most studies of institutional investor performance would not have been possible without the pioneering work in portfolio management of Dr. Harry M. Markowitz.[10] Markowitz developed the concept of "portfolio efficiency." This involves portfolios that satisfy the dual criteria of (1) highest expected return for a given level of risk, or (2) lowest level of risk for a given level of expected return. This leads to a family of portfolios called "efficient sets" or "efficient frontier." That is, if risk (variability of expected return) is measured and if covariance among securities is accounted for, the efficient set of portfolios is comprised of those combinations of securities in which, for a given amount of risk, there is no other portfolio that provides higher expected return. Conversely, for a given expected return there is no portfolio that carries less risk.

Figure 3-1 presents the efficient set, in which no other portfolio at risk level σ_j provides higher expected return than R_j. Portfolio J is efficient, as are all portfolios on the line of the efficient set.

Markowitz developed sophisticated mathematical techniques in order to obtain the efficient set. The application of his theory was all but impossible because of the extraordinary number of assessments

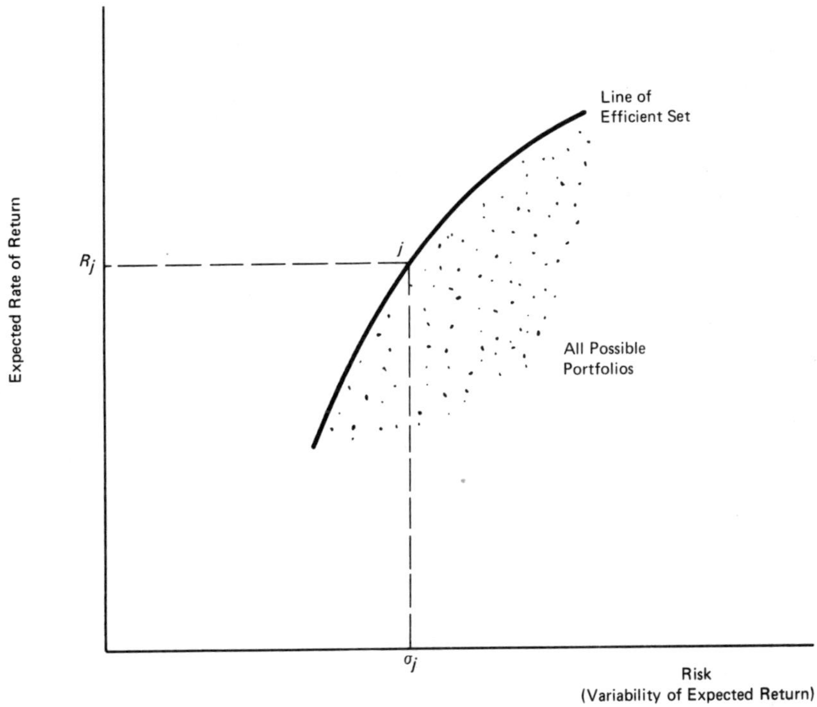

Figure 3-1. Markowitz's Efficient Set

involved. Markowitz suggested a means of substantially reducing the input requirement by making the additional assumption that security returns were jointly normal and related only through a common normally distributed market factor.[11]

William F. Sharpe simplified Markowitz's model into a usable form by utilizing the above assumption.[12] Sharpe suggested that, since all security returns are significantly correlated with the market as a whole, a satisfactory simplification would be to abandon the covariances of each security with each other security and to substitute information on the relationship of each security to the market (e.g., Standard and Poor's 500 Stock Index).

Risk Characteristics

Sharpe developed the capital asset pricing model, which states that the expected return on any asset (or portfolio) is related to both the riskless rate of return and the return on the market:[13]

$$E(R_j) = R^* + [E(R_m) - R^*]B_j$$

In this case R_j is the return on the asset (or portfolio), R^* is the return on a riskless asset, R_m is the return on the market, and B_j (the beta coefficient) is a measure of the sensitivity of the return on the asset (or portfolio) to movements in the market. The balance of the risk associated with the portfolio is unique to that portfolio. It is not priced by the market, since the combination of securities in efficient portfolios eliminates this residual risk. Thus, the risk that is unique to the security in a well-diversified portfolio is eliminated.[14]

The above equation deals with expected return on a portfolio. The relationship between the actual risk premium on an asset (the actual return minus the riskless rate of return) and returns on the market is represented by a regression equation derived from the above equation:

$$R_j - R^* = \alpha + B_j(R_m - R^*) + ej$$

In this model α and B_j are the intercept and slope terms, respectively, of a least square line, and *ej* is a random error term with zero mean (see Figure 3-2).

Michael C. Jensen was the first to fully develop and utilize this equation for the evaluation of institutional investor performance.[15] He studied the performance of 115 mutual funds over a 20-year period to determine whether their level of systematic risk (beta coefficient) in the portfolio was consistent with their rate of return.[16]

The reasoning behind Jensen's model suggests that, if the portfolio manager is a superior predictor of security prices, then the intercept term (α) will turn out to be positive. Moreover, when the regression is based upon past performance, α becomes a good method for ranking and comparing portfolio performance. Only systematic risk is considered in this performance measure, since residual risk in a well diversified portfolio is assumed to be zero.[17]

Since the late 1960s most institutional investor performance studies employed Jensen's or a variation of Jensen's model.[18] The alpha (α) term in his model becomes the composite performance measure. That is, if the performance measure (alpha) is positive, the fund has outperformed an unmanaged portfolio of similar risk. The higher the positive alpha, the better the risk-adjusted performance (see Figure 3-3). Conversely, if alpha is negative, this demonstrates

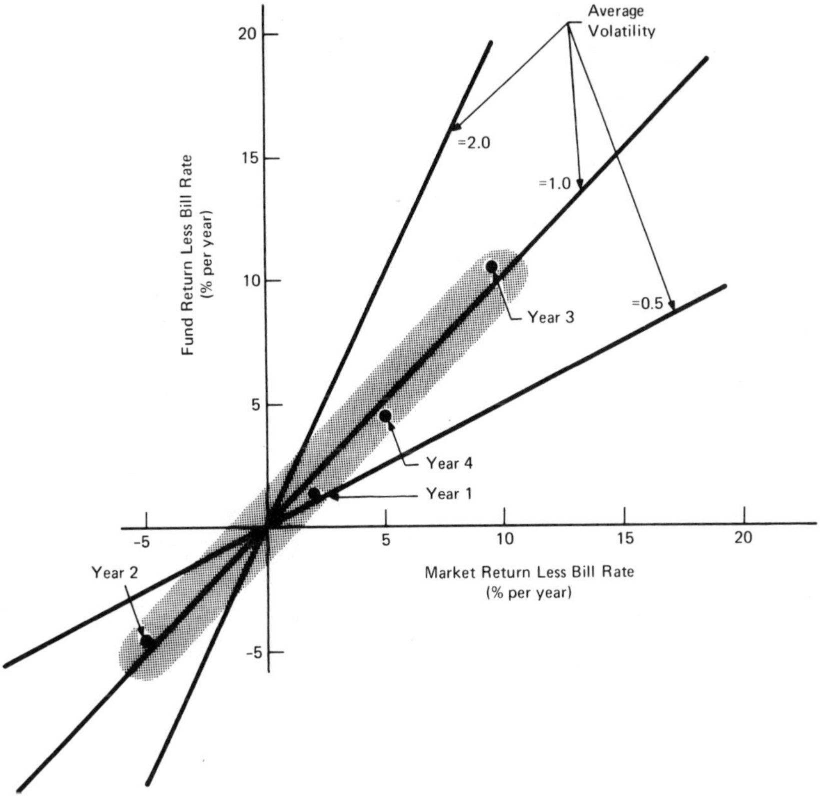

Figure 3-2. Measurement of Fund Volatility. Source: SEC, *Institutional Investor Study*, vol. 2 (1971), p. 407.

that the fund is not a superior selector of securities. More importantly, it shows that the fund did less well than an unmanaged portfolio of similar risk.

The performance model discussed above has been employed by a number of studies that are referred to later. Unfortunately, not all performance studies take risk into consideration, and this will be so stated in each case.

Institutional Stocks

Before we discuss in detail some major performance studies of pension funds and other institutional investors, it is appropriate to mention here a rather unusual index compiled by the investment

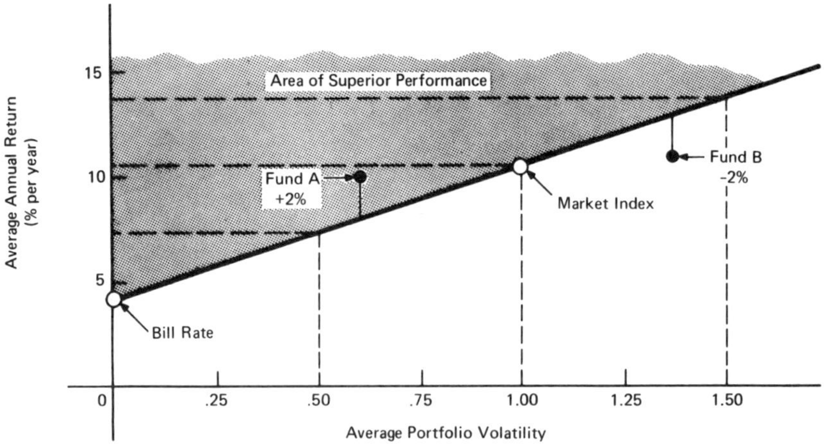

Figure 3-3. Evaluation of Fund Performance. Source: SEC, *Institutional Investor Study*, vol. 2 (1971), p. 406.

advisory firm of Piper, Jaffray, and Hopwood.[19] Steven C. Leuthold, creator of this index, found that it was not quite satisfactory to analyze institutional performance against the existing indices. Thus, he developed the Leuthold Institutional Index.[20] This index is subdivided into three broad tiers. The first tier is known as the classic institutional stocks: "These are the quality stocks most widely held by institutions. . . . The category runs from Aetna to Xerox. . . . This is not a super growth stock list."[21] The first tier index includes approximately one hundred of the most widely held common stocks.

The second group in the index is called the common institutional stocks: "These are 400 blue chip and pale blue chip companies. . . . Some of the components have a better quality and growth image than issues in Tier I, but they are smaller companies and not as widely held in institutional circles."[22] This second tier represents the majority of all institutional stock holdings.

The third tier—marginal institutional stocks—consists of companies that are on the fringe of the institutional universe.[23]

Thus, the Leuthold institutional index gives recognition to the fact that, because of size, quality, and preference considerations, the institutional universe of stocks does not consist of all available equities. Moreover, when the index is weighted, more weight is given to tier I securities than to tier II and greater weight to tier II than to tier III. This adjusts for the fact that the portfolio manager would consider major commitments to stocks in either tier I, II, or III quite differently.[24]

Table 3-1 distinctly demonstrates several points. First, it shows that even institutional favorites fluctuate differently over time. That is, each of the different institutional tiers had differing returns for the periods covered.

More importantly, from the point of view of performance, these institutional favorites did poorly. For all periods and in all cases, this institutional index and most subgroups did substantially more poorly than either Standard and Poor's 500 Stock Index or the Dow Jones Industrial Average. This includes the year 1972 when the Leuthold index return was 13.9 percent weighted and 11.8 percent unweighted, while the S & P 500 and the Dow Jones Industrials increased by 15.6 percent and 14.6 percent, respectively. The glaring differences are most apparent in down markets. For the years 1973 and 1974 the popular average significantly outperformed the weighted or unweighted institutional index.

This sort of performance during the last three years in no way indicates superior returns on the part of these professional investors. It would have been better investment strategy to purchase the equivalent of the Standard and Poor's 500 Stock Index.[25] This issue is probed more deeply in a later chapter.

Table 3-1
The Leuthold Institutional Index Compared with the Popular Averages

Performance	1972	1973	January 1, 1974 to August 8, 1974
Tier I (classic institutional stocks)	+19.6%	−15.2%	−16.1%
Tier II (common institutional stocks)	+10.7	−24.5	−18.4
Tier III (fringe institutional stocks)	+16.7	−31.9	−16.4
Weighted index	+13.9	−22.2	−17.5
Unweighted index	+11.8	−24.2	−17.7
Dow Jones Industrial Average	+14.6	−16.6	− 6.3
Standard and Poor's 500 Stock Index	+15.6	−17.4	−15.3
NYSE composite index	+14.3	−19.6	−16.5

Note: Includes dividends.

Source: *Perception Indices*, The Leuthold Group, Division of Piper, Jaffray and Hopwood, Inc., 1974, Minneapolis, Minnesota.

There are several companies that specialize in doing pension performance studies, a service that enables pensions to evaluate their portfolio managers.[26] In most cases these studies compare the performance (usually rate of return) of that specific pension against other pension funds, mutual funds, and the market averages. What follows is based upon a study completed by Callan Associates in which the performance of bank-pooled pension equity funds was analyzed against both other institutional investor performance and the market averages. All returns are time-weighted and are annualized rates of return, that is, they represent the average annual compounded rate of return including dividend reinvestment.

Pooled Equity Funds

Upon examination of Table 3-2 several points become immediately apparent. For the 10-year period ending June 30, 1974, the Standard and Poor's 500 Stock Index returned a mere 3.77 percent (dividends included). The return on the Dow Jones Industrials was just 3.35 percent. This return has certainly been greatly affected by the depressed market, which is still occurring at the end of 1974.

Table 3-2
Summary of Time-weighted Rates of Return, Cumulative Periods Ending June 30, 1974

	1 Year	3 Years	5 Years	7 Years	10 Years
Standard and Poor's 500 Stock Index	(14.54)	(1.79)	0.71	2.48	3.77
Dow Jones Industrial Average	(6.12)	0.22	2.13	2.76	3.35
Median rates of return					
Bank-pooled equity funds–I	(15.34)%	(3.69)%	0.15%	1.48%	3.30%
Bank-pooled equity funds–II	(14.42)	(3.80)	0.89	2.73	3.63
Insurance company separate accounts	(13.84)	(5.19)	(1.31)	0.54	3.09
Growth and income mutual funds	(11.28)	(4.13)	(0.84)	1.36	3.82
Growth mutual funds	(14.81)	(8.19)	(3.47)	(1.71)	3.95
Investment counselor equity portfolio	(8.56)	(1.30)	1.27	--	--
Mean return of institutional investor	(13.0417)	(4.3817)	(0.5517)	0.8800	3.558

Source: Callan Associates, Inc., San Francisco, California, 1974.

However, a surprising revelation presents itself when bank-pooled pension equity fund-I comes under close scrutiny. This Group I represents the larger banks in the country. Since Group I banks manage a larger pool of employee benefit plans than Group II, their performance is much more significant. For all periods–one, three, five, seven, and ten years–these pooled equity funds did more poorly than either the broader-based Standard and Poor's composite index or the narrower-based Dow Jones Industrial Average. Group I provided a 3.30 percent return for the 10-year period, as opposed to 3.77 percent for the Standard and Poor's 500 and 3.35 percent for Dow Jones Industrials. Looking to a more recent period, for the three years ending June 30, 1974, Group I bank-pooled equity funds did even more poorly relative to the popular market indices. Their return was a negative 3.68 percent for that period. In the latest year ending June 30, 1974, the entire equity market did poorly, but once again these pooled pensions in Group I did still more poorly.

An interesting comparison can now be made with Group II pooled funds, which manage a smaller amount of employee benefit funds. Invariably, these smaller institutions outperformed their more substantial colleagues in every period studied. A possible explanation for this could be that fund size and bank size are important factors affecting performance. As Dr. Friend states:

> Some loss in investment flexibility is associated with very large size. The need to purchase portfolio securities in very large blocks may take substantial amounts of time, so that investment opportunities are lost, and even in the short run may drive up the price of the securities involved beyond the level at which they were initially attractive. If the portfolio holdings are sufficiently large, the decision to sell may again take substantial time to implement, since the alternative could be a major break in the market for the issue.[27]

In essence, the key disadvantage to large fund size is that it seems to reduce investment flexibility. Unfortunately, in several recent studies of pension and mutual funds these theoretical considerations were not substantiated.[28] In fact, no relationship was found between fund performance and fund size.[29]

One other possible explanation is that there were significant differences in the risk levels assumed by Group I and Group II pooled funds. Although it was true that Group II had a slightly lower beta than Group I, this factor cannot fully explain the difference in their respective returns.[30] Further investigation into this area is strongly needed, since the implications of a possible negative relationship between fund size and performance are enormous. The eventual result would be to have a significant redistribution of pension funds to more numerous and smaller administrators. However, this possible relationship has not at all been proven and research must continue in this area.

An interesting corollary to this factor of fund size is the performance of equity oriented portfolios managed by investment counseling firms. These firms generally manage funds that are smaller in size than the bank group. As can be observed in Table 3-2, these managers outperformed all other institutional investors covered by this study for one-, three-, and five-year periods. They also outperformed the Standard & Poor's composite index for each of those three periods. This may be partly explained by the fact that their risk level, beta coefficient, was 0.96—slightly less than the market index and the other institutional funds. But again, this is only a partial answer, since size may have been an important factor also.

In further analyzing Table 3-2, it is seen that both insurance company separate (equity) accounts and growth mutual funds did particularly poorly for the one-, three-, five-, and seven-year periods. However, because of their higher risk level, these growth mutual funds outperformed all other categories of investors for the ten-year period. One possible explanation is that there was a strong bull market during the 1965-68 period.

In order to understand performance better, one must take into consideration the level of risk assumed in the portfolio and the return received for that risk level, for it is a general tenet of finance that over the long term, with higher risk, higher returns will ensue.[31] Conversely, with a lower risk level a rate of return lower than the market is assumed, and thus does not necessarily indicate inferior performance.

Tables 3-3 and 3-4 present the pertinent statistics on the performance of Group I and Group II pooled equity funds.[32] First, it is shown that the coefficient of determination (R^2) is 0.89 for Group I and 0.87 for Group II. This statistic is the degree of diversification in each particular portfolio. The 0.89 simply means that 89 percent of all the volatility of each return in the average portfolio can be explained by the movements of the market (e.g., Standard and Poor's composite index). Only 11 percent of the volatility is related to nonmarket factors such as movements of a particular security or

Table 3-3
Linear Regression Analysis, Five Years Ending June 30, 1974, Bank-pooled Equity Funds–Group I

	Alpha	Beta	Correlation Coefficient	Diversification Measure R^2	Five-years Time-weighted Annual Rate of Return	Excess Returns	Standard Deviation Ratio
1	0.2	1.14	0.942	0.8874	0.16%	–0.93	9.78
2	–0.6	1.04	0.927	0.8593	(2.27)	–1.64	9.04
3	–0.3	1.02	0.890	0.7921	(1.10)	–1.33	9.22
4	0.2	0.97	0.975	0.9506	1.41	–0.79	8.06
5	0.2	1.11	0.969	0.9390	0.65	–0.89	9.23
6	–0.1	0.98	0.977	0.9545	0.45	–1.02	8.11
7	–0.5	1.07	0.953	0.9082	(2.03)	–1.58	9.10
8	–0.6	1.20	0.955	0.9120	(3.04)	–1.73	10.14
9	–0.4	1.35	0.913	0.8336	(3.54)	–1.67	11.98
10	–0.1	1.03	0.973	0.9467	0.15	–1.07	8.53
11	0.3	1.09	0.956	0.9139	1.35	–0.72	9.19
12	–0.3	1.13	0.969	0.9390	(1.34)	–1.37	9.46
13	–0.4	0.85	0.910	0.8281	(0.18)	–1.23	7.57
14	0.1	1.09	0.927	0.8593	0.37	–0.92	9.54
15	–0.3	1.05	0.959	0.9197	(0.96)	–1.33	8.84
16	0.4	1.19	0.884	0.7815	0.50	–0.75	10.91
17	0.7	1.02	0.951	0.9044	3.32	–0.27	8.67
18	–0.5	1.09	0.946	0.8949	(1.88)	–1.52	9.34
19	0.1	0.84	0.979	0.9584	2.22	–0.68	6.95
20	–0.9	1.37	0.950	0.9025	(5.46)	–2.20	11.64
21	–0.7	1.12	0.904	0.8172	(3.37)	–1.82	10.06
22	–0.4	0.71	0.863	0.7448	0.75	–1.05	6.63
23	–0.3	1.01	0.950	0.9025	(2.57)	–1.75	8.61
24	0.1	1.07	0.945	0.8930	0.47	–0.94	9.19
25	–0.2	0.78	0.938	0.8798	1.19	–0.94	6.73
26	–1.1	1.02	0.949	0.9006	(3.97)	–2.10	8.70
27	0.5	1.05	0.940	0.8836	1.99	–0.56	9.07
28	0.1	1.25	0.922	0.8501	(1.09)	–1.15	10.93
29	–0.8	1.12	0.953	0.9082	(3.62)	–1.93	9.48
30	0.2	1.00	0.960	0.9216	1.24	–0.81	8.33
Mean	–0.9%	1.067	0.940	0.8862	0.6737	–1.23	1.139

Source: Callan Associates Inc., San Francisco, California, 1974.

Table 3-4
Linear Regression Analysis, Five Years Ending June 30, 1974, Bank-pooled Equity Funds–Group II

	Alpha	Beta	Correlation Coefficient	Diversification Measure R^2	Five-years Time-Weighted Annual Rate of Return	Excess Returns	Standard Deviation Ratio
1	0.1	0.97	0.886	0.6989	0.85%	–0.87	8.87
2	–0.6	1.07	0.967	0.9351	(2.12)	–1.60	8.92
3	0.3	1.11	0.970	0.9409	1.17	–0.75	9.26
4	0.6	0.91	0.991	0.9821	3.80	–0.26	7.39
5	–0.3	0.94	0.854	0.7293	(0.59)	–1.22	8.87
6	–1.9	0.95	0.925	0.8556	(6.79)	–2.86	8.33
7	–1.1	1.12	0.956	0.9139	(4.68)	–2.22	9.44
8	0.6	1.07	0.953	0.9082	2.65	–0.41	9.09
9	0.1	1.01	0.984	0.8723	0.89	–0.90	3.32
10	–0.8	0.73	0.927	0,8593	(1.10)	–1.54	6.40
11	–0.5	0.94	0.890	0.7921	(1.34)	–1.45	8.50
12	0.2	0.93	0.934	0.8723	1.74	–0.72	8.04
13	0.3	1.06	0.964	0.9292	1.42	–0.73	8.89
14	0.1	0.93	0.958	0.9370	1.38	–0.82	7.78
15	3.6	1.01	0.690	0.9216	14.32	2.59	11.82
16	–0.3	1.02	0.980	0.8649	0.43	–1.01	8.39
17	0.9	0.86	0.926	0.8574	5.05	0.06	7.52
18	–0.3	1.17	0.876	0.7673	(4.14)	–1.95	10.77
19	–0.7	0.92	0.924	0.8537	(1.75)	–1.59	8.01
20	0.3	1.36	0.935	0.8742	(0.96)	–1.03	11.75
21	0.6	1.17	0.981	0.9624	1.86	–0.54	9.66
Mean	0.0	1.01	0.981	0.8727	0.75	–0.53	9.79

Source: Callan Associates, Inc., San Francisco, California, 1974.

industry. Table 3-5 shows that the range of the degree of diversification is from 74 percent to 96 percent. This higher degree of diversification is generally expected for most large institutional portfolios.

Thus, since the market factor is the most important element in determining rates of return, individual stock selection tends to take a secondary role in portfolio management. What is of paramount importance is the selection of the risk level desired, since this will subsequently affect the rate of return to be obtained. As discussed earlier in this chapter, the risk level measurement most often used is

Table 3-5
Linear Regression Analysis, Five Years Ending June 30, 1974, Insurance Company Separate Accounts

	Alpha	Beta	Correlation Coefficient	Diversification Measure R^2	Five-years Time-weighted Annual Rate of Return	Excess Returns	Standard Deviation Ratio
1	−1.4	0.93	0.964	0.9293	(4.54)%	−2.31	3.23
2	−0.3	1.19	0.926	0.8575	(1.89)	−1.42	10.36
3	0.3	1.07	0.971	0.9428	3.62	−0.19	8.91
4	−0.9	1.17	0.924	0.8538	(4.36)	−2.06	10.20
5	−1.2	1.12	0.899	0.8082	(5.31)	−2.32	10.03
6	0.0	1.28	0.930	0.8649	(1.31)	−1.20	11.08
7	−0.9	0.79	0.943	0.8892	(1.63)	−1.64	5.77
8	−0.4	0.85	0.937	0.8780	0.00	−1.20	7.35
9	−1.2	1.23	0.920	0.8464	(6.01)	−2.42	10.32
10	−0.4	0.99	0.991	0.9821	(0.82)	−1.35	8.08
11	−0.1	1.15	0.940	0.8836	(0.85)	−1.18	9.91
12	−1.2	1.11	0.949	0.8911	(4.94)	−2.28	9.48
13	−0.1	0.89	0.915	0.8372	0.67	−1.00	7.84
14	0.1	1.29	0.955	0.9120	(1.26)	−1.19	10.92
Mean	−0.55	1.04	0.938	0.8840	(2.045)	−1.61	9.39

Source: Callan Associates, Inc., San Francisco, California, 1974.

the beta coefficient, which measures the level of sensitivity of the portfolio to the market. A portfolio with a beta coefficient of 1.0 should generally track the performance of the market. Also included in Tables 3-5 and 3-6 is the standard deviation about the mean return. This measurement is very similar to the beta coefficient in highly diversified portfolios.

In analyzing the beta coefficient, one finds that both Group I and Group II pooled equity funds have slightly higher betas than the market. Looking at alpha, the performance measure, one finds that the mean alpha for Group I funds is –0.2. This indicates that, on average, these funds earned –0.2 percent less per year (in this five-year period of study) than they should have for their level of systematic risk (beta). It is clear that the distribution is skewed to the low side since 18 funds had negative alphas, while only 13 had positive ones.

The performance is slightly different for Group II, the smaller

Table 3-6
Linear Regression Analysis, Five Years Ending June 30, 1974, Growth Mutual Funds

	Alpha	Beta	Correlation Coefficient	Diversification Measure R^2	Excess Returns	Standard Deviation Ratio
1	−3.5	1.33	0.852	0.7430	−4.81	12.45
2	−2.2	1.35	0.911	0.8299	−3.51	12.07
3	−1.8	1.34	0.906	0.8208	−3.15	11.95
4	−1.3	1.71	0.906	0.8208	−3.43	15.24
5	1.0	0.90	0.911	0.8299	0.11	8.00
6	−2.5	1.45	0.930	0.8649	−3.93	12.60
7	−1.3	1.05	0.939	0.8817	−2.27	9.05
8	−0.9	1.15	0.938	0.8798	−2.05	9.87
9	0.1	1.14	0.920	0.8464	−0.96	10.01
10	−0.5	1.26	0.886	0.7850	−1.70	11.53
11	−0.3	1.12	0.925	0.8556	−1.88	9.80
12	−0.4	0.32	0.856	0.7327	−1.27	3.67
13	−0.1	0.96	0.937	0.8780	−1.04	8.31
14	0.3	1.24	0.914	0,8353	−0.95	10.99
15	−2.3	1.24	0.891	0.9624	−3.50	11.25
16	−2.8	1.07	0.820	0.6724	−3.85	10.55
17	−1.9	1.00	0.806	0.6496	−2.84	10.02
18	−1.2	1.32	0.918	0.8427	−2.45	11.64
19	−0.5	1.16	0.910	0.8281	−1.60	10.33
20	0.3	1.23	0.927	0.8593	−0.88	10.72
21	−0.6	0.97	0.961	0.9235	−1.56	8.20
22	−0.6	1.16	0.977	0.9545	−1.72	9.61
23	−0.3	1.03	0.917	0.8409	−1.77	9.09
24	−0.6	1.27	0.885	0.7832	−1.86	11.53
25	−0.4	1.48	0.836	0.6989	−1.84	13.45
26	−0.5	1.08	0.917	0.8409	−1.52	9.49
27	−1.4	1.54	0.814	0.6626	−2.89	15.31
28	−0.6	1.03	0.892	0.7956	−1.69	9.73
Mean	−1.03	1.21	0.90	0.8185	−2.10	10.90

Source: Callan Associates, Inc., San Francisco, California, 1974.

bank-administered funds. Here the mean performance alpha is zero, which is the level expected given the risk taken. But more importantly, the distribution here is skewed to the high side with two-thirds of the funds having positive alphas while only one-third were negative.

This demonstrates that there were only a few funds that did particularly poorly in Group II. However, the mean alpha was reduced to zero due to these few poor performers. The median performance (alpha) is positive and this tends to demonstrate that for the five-year period ending June 30, 1974, these bank-pooled equity funds performed better than would have been expected from the level of risk taken. Therefore, these funds showed a slightly superior equity performance record for this period.[33]

In order to understand pooled equity fund performance better, the author analyzed whether or not there is any relationship between risk (beta) and performance. The results of this analysis show a slight inverse relationship between risk and return during the five-year period ending June 30, 1974. However, this was not found to be statistically significant.[34] As can be seen from the scatter diagram, Figure 3-4, there seems to be a slight negative relationship between

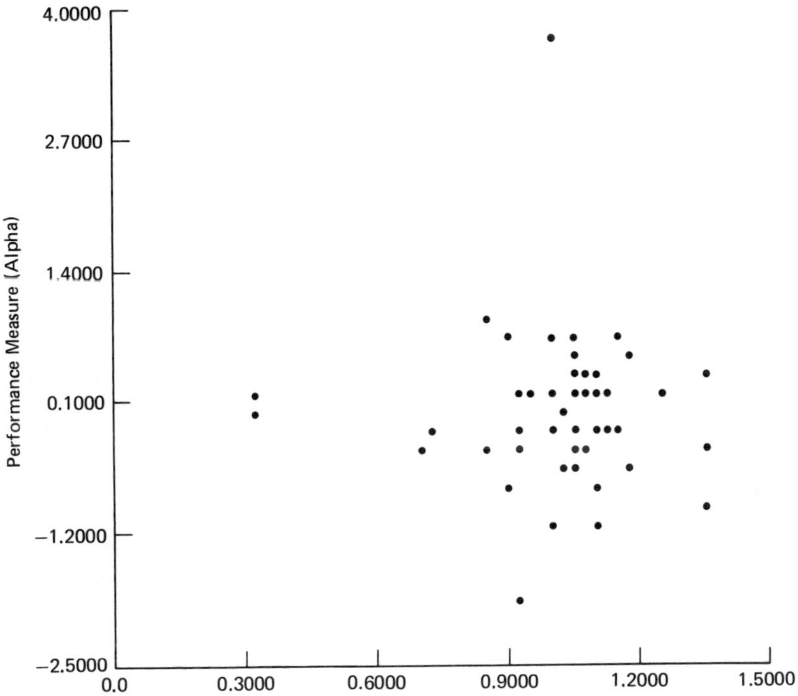

Figure 3-4. Relationship Between the Beta Coefficient (Risk) and the Performance Measure (Alpha) for the Five-year Period Ending June 30, 1974, for Bank-administered, Pooled Equity Funds. Source: Derived from Tables 3-3 and 3-4.

risk (beta) and performance (alpha). That is, at higher levels of risk the level of performance decreased and at lower levels of risk the performance improved. One possible explanation may be that during most of this period the market performed poorly and the more conservative portfolios, as classified by their risk level, out-performed their riskier rivals.[35] Interestingly enough, this author found the exact opposite in a study of bank administered commingled pension funds for the 1962-70 period. These findings showed that risk-adjusted performance was positively related to the level of risk (beta).[36] There seem to be no consistent results in this area. Again, further research is needed.

Insurance Company Accounts

As is seen in Table 3-5, insurance company separate equity accounts did particularly poorly for the five-year period ending June 30, 1974. Several factors are immediately evident. First, just as the bank-pooled funds, these separate accounts are also highly diversified. Looking at the coefficient of determination (R^2), which signifies the level of diversification, we find the mean R^2 equal to 0.88, that is, 88 percent of the changes in these portfolios can be explained by movements in the market.

Also, these insurance company separate accounts generally have a slightly higher risk level than the bank-pooled funds previously discussed. Here the mean beta equals 1.08 with a range of 0.79 to 1.29.

The main element is not the risk level, nor is it the degree of diversification. What is of prime importance is whether or not the portfolio received sufficient return for the risk taken. Analyzing the performance measure, one finds that alpha is –0.5%. This translates that, on average, these separate equity accounts received a 0.5% lower return than an unmanaged portfolio with similar risk would have returned.

Briefly analyzing Table 3-6 one finds that, as would be expected, the growth oriented mutual funds maintained a substantially higher risk level than the other institutions discussed. The mean beta coefficient for these mutuals equals 1.20. Thus, on the average these funds held 20 percent more risk in their portfolios than did the market in general. The range is from 0.90 to 1.71.

The basic objective of the growth mutuals is the willingness to take higher risk in order to attain accompanying higher returns. If the rates of return proved to be commensurate with the risk taken, then this objective would be achieved. Unfortunately, Table 3-6 demonstrates that the mean performance measure was −1 percent for the five-year period ending June 30, 1974. This means that they not only performed more poorly than the previously discussed institutions, but, more importantly from the investor's standpoint, their goals were definitely not attained.

Investment Counselors

The last group of institutional investors to be analyzed for the same five-year period are investment counselors. This group is important since in recent years many pensions seem to be splitting the management of their funds and investment counselors have been among those who have profited from this trend (see Table 3-7).[37] One reason often given for this occurrence is the greater flexibility that these accounts have over the larger bank-administered accounts.

The results show that these funds have a very high degree of diversification, as evidenced by an R^2 of 0.92. Also, the level of risk taken is, in general, slightly less than the market. The range is rather wide, going from a beta of 0.70 to 1.20. However, the most

Table 3-7
Linear Regression Analysis, Five Years Ending June 30, 1974, Investment Counselor Equity Portfolios

	Alpha	Beta	Correlation Coefficient	Diversification Measure R^2	Five-years Time-weighted Annual Rate of Return	Excess Returns	Standard Deviation Ratio
A	0.1	0.93	0.921	0.8482	--	−0.82	8.20
B	0.1	0.70	0.976	0.9526	--	−0.58	5.76
C	0.2	1.20	0.959	0.9197	0.19	−0.92	10.14
D	0.1	0.89	0.966	0.9331	1.66	−0.78	7.43
E	0.0	1.10	0.973	0.9467	0.01	−1.05	9.12
Mean	0.1	0.96	0.959	0.9201	0.62	−0.83	8.13

Source: Callan Associates, Inc., San Francisco, California, 1974.

important factor is the risk-adjusted performance. The performance measure, alpha, is 0.1 percent. Furthermore, not one of the funds had a negative alpha during the five-year period. These findings must be weighed in light of the fact that the sample included only six investment counselors. This may bias the results since perhaps only those counselors who did well chose to participate in this study. However, for all periods they outperformed Standard and Poor's 500 Stock Index. For the last one-year period, 47 investment counselors participated, while for the three-year period there were 25 funds involved.[38]

What must now be concluded from this study of the institutional investor is that, with the exception of investment counselors, those institutions studied definitely did not perform as well as an unmanaged portfolio with similar risk. This finding, which has been obtained in other studies, makes it clear that a randomly selected portfolio approximating the market risk would have been a superior performer. Some have suggested the use of market index funds whose objective would be to match the market return.[39] These results also tend to confirm the random walk theory, which states that market movements are random and that no one can consistently predict security prices.[40]

This author recently analyzed 37 bank-pooled equity funds for employee benefit plans for the 1962-70 period. The results tended to substantiate the findings of the previously discussed Callan Associates study.[41] The methodology employed was similar to that utilized and recommended by the Securities and Exchange Commission in their *Institutional Investors Study,*[42] that is, risk-adjusted performance was measured and the beta coefficient was used as a surrogate for risk.

The results were quite disturbing from the standpoints of effective portfolio management and allocation of financial resources. This study found that, on average, during the 1962-70 period these commingled equity funds provided a rate of return that was 1.6 percent worse per annum than an unmanaged portfolio (a naive buy and hold strategy) with similar risk.[43] In fact, of these 37 funds, 30 did worse than a totally unmanaged portfolio with a similar risk component. Moreover, even though seven funds had superior performance relative to an unmanaged portfolio of similar risk, none was superior by a statistically significant margin, that is, chance alone could have accounted for these seven funds' superior performance.

The 30 funds that did worse than the comparison portfolio did so by a statistically significant margin. Here, chance alone could not have accounted for this inferior performance.

Table 3-8 presents the distribution of risk-adjusted performance for the study period. Clearly, this performance measure, alpha, represents the average incremental rate of return on the portfolio, which is solely based upon the portfolio managers' ability to forecast security prices. The findings of this study point to their inability to adequately forecast these prices.

As can be seen from Table 3-9, the mean beta coefficient is 0.96, which indicates that the average commingled fund studied had slightly less risk than the market. The maximum and minimum beta are, respectively, 1.17 and 0.70. Thus, during this nine-year period these pooled equity funds did not take excessive risks in their equity portfolios.

Tables 3-10 and 3-11 show that the banks studied cut across many geographic areas. They also include banks of many different sizes.

Another significant finding is that there is no relationship between performance one year (or period) and performance during the following year (or period).[44] This indicates that there is no consistency in fund performance and that no one has a clear crystal ball.

In order to understand performance better, this author analyzed

Table 3-8
Distribution of Performance Measure–Alpha Period, January 1, 1962, Through September 30, 1970

Performance Measure Alpha	Number of Funds	Mean Alpha
Alpha 4% or above	1	+6.3%
Less than 4% and greater than zero	6	+1.2%
Less than zero and greater than –4%	28	–2.1%
–4% or less	2	–5.7%
Total	37	–1.6%

Mean alpha = –1.6%
Maximum alpha = +6.3%
Minimum alpha = –6.1%

Source: Malca, Edward, *Bank-Administered, Commingled Pension Funds: Performance & Characteristics, 1962-1970* (Lexington, Massachusetts: Lexington Books, D.C. Heath and Company, 1973), p. 43.

Table 3-9
Distribution of Volatility Measure (Beta) by Size Class[a]

Assets (in Millions of Dollars)	No. of Funds	(a)	(b)	(c)	Average Beta[b]
Less than $5	6	2	4	—	0.84
$5 and less than $25	8	—	6	2	0.95
$15 and less than $25	9	3	3	3	0.95
$25 and less than $45	4	—	1	3	1.04
$45 and above	6	—	1	5	1.07
Totals	33	5	15	13	0.96

Note:

(a) 0.70 ⩽ beta < 0.85; (b) 0.85 ⩽ beta < 1.0; (c) 1.0 ⩽ beta < 1.2; mean beta coefficient = 0.96; maximum beta coefficient = 1.17; minimum beta coefficient = 0.70.

[a]Size classification based upon total assets as of end of year 1970.

[b]Based upon unweighted arithmetic means of funds within each size classification.

Source: Malca, Edward, *Bank-Administered, Commingled Pension Funds: Performance and Characteristics, 1962-1970* (Lexington, Massachusetts: Lexington Books, D.C. Heath and Company, 1973), p. 42.

Table 3-10
Size Classification of Participating Banks, Based Upon Total Deposits on December 31, 1970

Assets (in Millions of Dollars)	Banks		Total Deposits (in Millions of Dollars)	
	Number	Percent	Amount	Percent
Below $300	7	18.9	1,518	1.3
$300 and less than $550	7	18.9	3,151	2.7
$550 and less than $1,200	10	27.0	7,765	6.7
$1,200 and less than $5,000	6	16.2	15,232	13.1
$5,000 and above	7	18.9	87,466	76.0
Total	37	100%	115,132	100%

Range of participating banks–total deposits December 31, 1970: Largest bank–$25.6 billion; smallest bank–$104 million; mean bank size–$3.2 billion.

Source: Malca, Edward, *Bank-Administered, Commingled Pension Funds: Performance and Characteristics, 1962-1970* (Lexington, Massachusetts: Lexington Books, D.C. Heath and Company, 1973), p. 20.

Table 3-11
Distribution of 37 Participating Banks by State

State	Number of Banks
Alabama	2
California	5
Colorado	2
Connecticut	1
Delaware	2
Hawaii	1
Illinois	1
Indiana	1
Maine	1
Maryland	1
Massachusetts	2
Minnesota	1
Missouri	2
Nebraska	2
New Mexico	1
New York	5
Ohio	2
Pennsylvania	4
Texas	1
Total number of participating banks	37

Source: Malca, Edward, *Bank-Administered, Commingled Pension Funds: Performance and Characteristics, 1962-1970* (Lexington, Massachusetts: Lexington Books, D.C. Heath and Company, 1973), p. 20.

several variables that may affect it: (a) bank size, (b) fund size, (c) turnover rates, and (d) risk. It was found that bank size had no relationship to performance. Even though the larger banks had more substantial research staffs, this advantage did not significantly improve their ability to forecast the market. Fund size and turnover rates were also not found to be important variables affecting performance.[45] Only risk–beta–was found to be positively correlated with risk-adjusted performance for this period.[46] That is, the greater the risk level assumed, the higher the performance achieved. This finding was not consistent in all time periods.[47]

Since New York City banks command a leading position in the

administration of private pensions, their mean performance was tested to determine whether or not they out-performed banks outside New York City. The author found that there was no significant difference between performance of New York City banks and performance of those banks outside New York City.[48] This indicates that the New York banks administer the majority of pension trust assets for reasons other than performance. Perhaps these factors include proximity to many corporate headquarters, "old-line" ties, or advantageous commercial lending arrangements.

The study under discussion did not take management fees into consideration, which means that the actual return would have been even lower than indicated. One possible shortcoming is that performance was measured after commission costs, while for the returns on the market no commissions were included. This may not be unrealistic, since these funds do have the option to buy and hold. However, they trade on the assumption that they can do better than a buy and hold strategy. Thus, it is legitimate to compare these funds against a naive buy and hold approach since most funds have that option.

Partly in response to congressional pressure for greater disclosure and partly for competitive reasons, most large New York City banks now release some information on the performance of their pooled equity funds for employee benefit plans.[49] The implied assumption tends to be that these funds adequately represent the average performance of the equity portion of pension funds.

In a recent *New York Times* article there was an analysis of the compounded annual rates of return for the major New York City banks.[50] Table 3-12 presents the annual rates of return, including income reinvested, for the leading New York City banks (for Bankers Trust, income is excluded). During the entire 12-year period only one bank, Morgan Guaranty Trust, had a mean performance that was superior to the Standard and Poor's 500 Stock Index. But in 1973 even Morgan did more poorly than the S & P 500. None of the other banks for which complete data are available matched the market performance for the 12-year period.

The aforementioned article does not take risk into consideration, whereas one possible reason for Morgan's superior rate of return may indeed be related to higher risk levels. Moreover, the other banks may have substantially lower risk levels to account for their poorer returns. This does not seem very plausible, however, since most studies of pooled equity funds point to the fact that their risk levels (beta) tend to approximate that of the market.[51]

Table 3-12
Annual Rates of Return in Commingled Equity Funds for Employee Benefit Plans

	Income Reinvested						Exclude Income	
	Chase	Chemical	Citibank	Mfg. Hanover	Morgan	S & P 500	Bankers	S & P 500
1962	−11.24	−12.60	N.A.	−14.40	−15.1	−8.83	−16.50	−11.81
1963	20.49	22.34	N.A.	18.77	24.7	22.50	19.78	18.89
1964	12.50	15.58	N.A.	12.60	17.0	16.30	7.81	12.97
1965	16.52	13.53	14.96	10.37	17.6	12.27	9.48	9.06
1966	−4.88	−0.62	−5.31	−8.40	−6.9	−9.99	−9.96	−13.09
1967	26.08	23.25	21.73	24.36	26.2	23.73	20.63	20.09
1968	4.95	10.63	1.04	11.05	6.0	10.84	3.16	7.66
1969	−9.86	−11.41	7.08	1.34	−0.2	−8.32	−5.37	−11.36
1970	−3.97	−11.00	−8.93	−8.80	0.1	3.51	−20.07	0.10
1971	15.10	25.90	22.80	22.80	18.5	14.35	0.01[a]	+2.85[a]
1972	6.50	11.40	22.40	25.10	25.8	18.99		
1973	−17.90	−16.30	−18.30	−20.20	−20.8	−14.67		
12-year mean compounded annual rate of return 1962-73	+3.65	+4.85	5.38[b]	+5.11	+6.6	+5.87		

[a]Compounded annual rate of return for nine years (1962-70) without reinvestment of income.

[b]Compounded annual return for nine years (1965-73).

N.A. = Not available.

Source: "Market Place," *New York Times*, April 23, 1974. © 1974 by The New York Times Company. Reprinted by permission.

Table 3-13 shows the performance of New York City banks during the three-year period ending December 31, 1973. They did substantially better than they had during the previous 12-year period. Of the nine banks involved, seven did better than the market while only two did more poorly for this three-year time span. Almost all did quite poorly in 1973, but their superior performance during the previous two years more than made up for this poor showing.

The rate of return for the special situation pooled equity funds should be noted in the last column of Table 3-13. These are generally the more aggressive funds specializing in smaller, more rapidly expanding companies. They are willing to assume additional risk in order to obtain expected higher returns.[52] Since 1973 was a depressed year for the stock market, the rates of return for these special situation funds reflected even greater losses than the market. The minimum loss was 25 percent while the maximum loss was over 43 percent. In fact, in 1973 the mean return for these aggressive funds was –35 percent, which was more than double the loss on the Standard and Poor's 500 Stock Index. It seems quite unlikely that

Table 3-13
Annual Equity Rates of Return for New York Bank-administered Commingled Funds, 1971-73

	Year			Three-year Compounded Return	Special Situation Return Year 1973
	1971	1972	1973		
Bank of New York	19.50%	19.70%	–11.2%	8.3%	–25.10
Bankers Trust	25.10	20.50	–28.4	2.6	–39.30
Chase	15.10	6.50	–17.9	0.2	–30.45
Chemical	25.90	11.40	–16.3	5.5	–23.90
Citibank	22.80	25.40	–18.3	7.1	–32.50
Irving Trust	18.80	22.50	–18.4	7.1	–38.54
Manufacturer's Hanover	22.80	25.10	–20.2	7.0	–43.44
Morgan Guaranty	18.10	25.90	–20.8	5.6	–39.46
U.S. Trust	28.40	21.90	–22.9	6.5	–42.00
S & P 500	14.35	18.99	–14.7	5.0	Mean return 1973: –35.0

Note: Includes reinvestment of dividends.

Source: "Market Place," *New York Times*, January 23, 1974. © 1974 by The New York Times Company. Reprinted by permission.

the risk levels on these special funds were more than double that of the market. Therefore, on the basis of risk adjusted performance, these funds also probably did poorly.

Thus, from all indications New York City banks were not superior selectors of common stock.[53] It is true that for the three-year period ending December 31, 1973, their performance was quite good, but this may be due to chance.

In order to obtain a better understanding of the equity performance of New York City bank trust departments, there will follow an in-depth analysis of one of the leading New York City banks. This bank has eight different commingled funds for employee benefit plans, including three equity funds. These equity funds are comprised of a common stock fund, an intermediate capitalization fund, and a special situation fund. The total assets in trust at this New York City bank are in excess of $20 billion.

Table 3-14 presents the time-weighted annual rates of return for the bank's commingled equity fund. This fund had roughly $500 million in assets at the end of 1973. It has been in existence since 1956 and the compounded rate of return was 9.3 percent from January 1, 1957 to the end of 1973. However, if the period had begun with 1966, 1968, or 1970, the return would have been 4.9 percent, 3.8 percent, and 4.3 percent, respectively. Of course, this is due to the fact that during the late 1960s and early 1970s the equities market did not perform very well.

Tables 3-15 and 3-16 present the returns of the other two pooled equity funds. The intermediate capitalization equity fund specializes in investing in medium-sized companies, while the special situation fund emphasizes the smaller, higher risk companies. As can be seen by the rate of return statistics, both of these two funds tend to take greater risk than the other pooled equity fund.

In recognition of the fact that rates of return are generally only significant over complete market cycles, Table 3-17 presents the performance of two pooled funds during different market cycles. The special situation fund did better than the other equity fund because of the higher risk assumed. Unfortunately, the level of risk assumed by each fund is not available, and thus a complete comparison between these two funds is not really possible.

The last table in this group is Table 3-18, which presents a very interesting comparison. It shows the returns achieved by the actual portion of common stock in pooled employee benefit plans. That is,

Table 3-14
Commingled Pension Trust Fund Common Stocks, Larger Companies (Time-weighted Annual Rates of Return, with Income Reinvested)

		Compounded Annually Over Period:	
	For Each Year	1/1/57 to End of Each Year	1/1 Each Year to 12/31/73
1957	−7.4%	−7.4%	9.3%
1958	43.5	15.3	10.4
1959	14.1	14.9	8.5
1960	6.9	12.9	8.1
1961	29.9	16.1	8.2
1962	−15.1	10.2	6.6
1963	24.7	12.2	8.8
1964	17.0	12.8	7.3
1965	17.6	13.3	6.2
1966	−6.9	11.1	4.9
1967	26.2	12.4	6.8
1968	6.0	11.8	3.8
1969	−0.2	10.9	3.4
1970	0.1	10.1	4.3
1971	18.5	10.6	5.7
1972	25.8	11.5	−0.2
1973	−20.8	9.3	−20.8

Note: Fund was established May 31, 1956.
Source: 1973 Annual Report of a leading New York City bank.

the table presents the results of the portions that were put into each of the three different equity funds for those pension funds whose common stock portfolios consist exclusively of commingled funds. The results seem to be very impressive, indeed. For every five- and ten-year period as well as for the entire period, 1961-73, the median equity performance of these funds was always superior to the Standard and Poor's composite index. This bank is either a superior predictor of security prices or its funds generally had a higher risk level than the Standard and Poor's index. The latter is the most plausible, for as one veteran Wall Street analyst explained:

> Very few men of real genius can be relied upon to do this (better performance) successfully over any length of time . . . much less any investment committee (referring to the investment committees of bank trust departments). . . .[54]

Table 3-15
Commingled Pension Trust Fund Intermediate Capitalization Equities (Time-weighted Annual Rates of Return, with Income Reinvested)

		Compounded Annually Over Period:	
	For Each Year	1/1/70 to End of Each Year	1/1 Each Year to 12/31/73
1970	8.1%	8.1%	2.0%
1971	31.0	19.0	0.1
1972	9.7	15.8	–12.5
1973	–30.3	2.0	–30.3

Note: Fund was established April 30, 1969.
Source: 1973 Annual Report of a leading New York City bank.

Table 3-16
Commingled Pension Trust Fund Special Situation Investments–Equities (Time-weighted Annual Rates of Return, with Income Reinvested)

		Compounded Annually Over Period:	
	For Each Year	1/1/65 to End of Each Year	1/1 Each Year to 12/31/63
1965	33.7%	33.7%	11.3%
1966	1.8	16.7	8.8
1967	68.8	31.9	9.9
1968	23.6	29.8	2.3
1969	–6.3	21.6	–1.5
1970	–18.6	13.7	–0.3
1971	58.9	19.3	6.7
1972	26.1	20.1	–12.6
1973	–39.4	11.3	–39.4

Note: Prior to establishment in its present form, November 30, 1964, the fund included convertible securities in addition to common stocks. From its original formation on January 31, 1961, it had annual rates of return of 48.9 percent for the 11 months to December 31, 1961; –20.1 percent for the year 1962; 12.0 percent for 1963; 10.0 percent for the 11 months to November 30, 1964.
Source: 1973 Annual Report of a leading New York City bank.

College Retirement Equities Fund

The final performance analysis of this chapter provides a thorough examination of a retirement fund that was considerably ahead of its

Table 3-17
Performance During Stock Market Cycles (Time-weighted Annual Rates of Return, Compounded Annually Over Cycle Period, with Income Reinvested)

	Commingled Pension Trust Funds			
	Months in Cycle	Common Stocks	Special Situation Equities	S & P Composite Index (500 Stocks)
Low-to-Low Cycles				
Oct. 31, 1960, to June 30, 1962	20	2.5%	—	4.7%
June 30, 1962, to Sept. 30, 1966	51	13.2	—	11.7
Sept. 30, 1966, to June 30, 1966	45	4.4	8.0%	1.9
June 30, 1970, to Dec. 31, 1973[a]	42	11.9	15.0	12.2
High-to-High Cycles				
Dec. 31, 1961, to Jan. 31, 1966	49	10.1	—	10.0
Jan. 31, 1966, to Nov. 30, 1968	34	8.9	29.9	9.1
Nov. 30, 1968, to Dec. 31, 1972	49	9.2	9.8	5.5

[a]Standard and Poor's Composite Index (500 stocks) on which cycle dates are based has declined further since December 31, 1973.

Source: 1973 Annual Report of a leading New York City bank.

time. The Teachers Insurance and Annuity Association (TIAA) was established in 1918 to provide fixed dollar retirement funds for its participants. Participants include colleges, universities, and certain other nonprofit and tax-exempt educational organizations. In 1952 TIAA formed a companion organization, College Retirement Equities Fund (CREF), which provides variable annuity benefits based upon common stock investment results. There are over 420,000 participants, and they may allocate their premium payments between TIAA and CREF in any proportion. The purpose of the joint income-variable income system is to provide a retirement income that is more responsive to economic change. The total assets of TIAA-CREF as of December 31, 1973, were $5.97 billion.[55] The total assets of CREF alone as of the end of 1973 were over $2.5 billion, which is the equivalent of one of the largest mutual funds. In fact, the $5.97 billion managed by TIAA-CREF constitutes what is probably the largest retirement fund, outside of state or local governments, that is independently managed.[56] Also, since its inception it has provided immediate vesting and portability for its participants. These concepts are just beginning to be accepted in the corporate pension field.

Table 3-18
Median Performance: Trusts with Common Stock Portion Wholly in Commingled Funds[a]

	Rate for Year		Makeup of Median (% in Each Commingled Fund)			Rate for Five Years			Rate for 10 Years			Rate for Total Period		
	Median	S & P 500	Common Stocks	Special Situation Equities	Intermediate Capitalization Equities		Median	S & P 500		Median	S & P 500		Median	S & P 500
1961	29.7%	26.8%	100.0%	—	—	1961-65	13.6%	13.2%	1961-70	9.0%	8.1%	1961-73	8.2%	7.4%
1962	–15.3	–8.8	97.1	2.9%	—	1962-66	6.3	5.6	1962-71	8.4	7.0			
1963	24.7	22.7	97.8	2.2	—	1963-67	15.4	12.3	1963-72	12.7	9.9			
1964	17.1	16.3	98.8	1.2	—	1964-68	11.9	10.1	1964-73	7.4	6.0			
1965	17.7	12.4	98.5	1.5	—	1965-69	8.3	4.9						
1966	–6.8	–10.1	98.4	1.6	—	1966-70	4.7	3.3						
1967	27.5	24.0	96.0	4.0	—	1967-71	10.5	8.4						
1968	6.9	11.0	93.9	6.1	—	1968-72	10.1	7.5						
1969	–0.2	–8.3	90.1	7.3	2.6%	1969-73	3.1	2.0						
1970	–0.8	4.0	89.0	7.0	4.0									
1971	22.2	14.3	85.1	8.9	6.0									
1972	25.0	19.0	84.6	9.2	6.2									
1973	–22.8	–14.8	88.3	6.2	5.5									

[a]The rates shown in this table are time-weighted annual rates of return. Rates for periods of more than one year are compounded annually. The median rate shown for each year or longer period is the rate achieved by the trust or trusts located at the median, in terms of common stock performance, among all employee benefit trusts whose common stock portion consisted entirely of units in commingled funds managed by the Trust and Investment Division. Stated another way, the number of trusts performing better than the median in the period was the same as the number performing less well. The S & P rates shown for the purpose of comparison are derived from Standard and Poor's Composite Index (500 Stocks). Both the median and the S & P rates of return assume investment of income. The percentage of the common stock portion invested in each commingled fund is as of the end of the year.

Source: 1973 Annual Report of a leading New York City bank.

Table 3-19 presents the average annual rate of return for CREF during the period 1953-73, which is 7.19 percent, based on a fixed monthly premium paid. Obviously, the compounded rate of return would be significantly less than the 7.19 percent indicated.

Some interesting findings emerge from a thorough analysis of CREF. First, this fund is very highly diversified with a coefficient of determination of 0.94. This means that 94 percent of the volatility of the fund can be explained by movements in the market. Secondly, the volatility risk level, beta, is equal to 1.10 for the 1957-73 period. That is, this fund tends to have 10 percent more risk than the market in general.

In order to obtain a better understanding of risk and return, the risk-adjusted performance is presented in Table 3-20. It can be seen that CREF's performance, alpha, is –0.10 percent on a quarterly basis, or approximately –0.40 percent on an annual basis. For the 1957-73 period, this fund did roughly 0.4 percent more poorly per annum than an unmanaged portfolio with similar risk would have done. One possible explanation for this difference could be that commission costs were not computed for the comparison standard. This negative alpha continued for two intraperiods. From 1957 to 1968 it was –0.44 percent per annum, and from 1969 to 1973 the alpha was –0.36 percent per annum. The consistency of this poor performance may be due, in part, to the commission costs incurred. The risk-adjusted performance shows some improvement for the later period 1969-73, and this may be explained by the fact that

Table 3-19
Average Annual Rates of Return for Periods Ending December 31[a] for College Retirement Equities Fund (CREF), 1957-73

Year Premiums Began (Jan. 1)	1957	1962	1967	1972	1973
1953	10.52%	9.62%	11.18%	9.52%	7.19%
1958		3.44	9.86	9.39	5.29
1963			10.97	8.49	3.82
1968				10.43	1.46
1973					–9.03

[a]These tables show CREF's past investment experience and should not be considered a prediction of CREF's performance for the years ahead.

Source: *CREF Investment Report 1973*, College Retirement Equities Fund, New York, 1974, p. 7.

commission costs became negotiable, probably reducing costs to CREF.

The mean excess return represents the return for the risk taken. That is, the actual rate of return is reduced by the three-month treasury bill rate, which is the risk-free rate of return (see Table 3-20). All funds had a positive mean excess return for the entire period 1957-73 (see Figures 3-5, 3-6, and 3-7). CREF had a return of approximately 4 percent per annum for the risk taken. During the intraperiod 1957-68, the mean excess return for CREF was approximately 7 percent per annum. This changed drastically during the last period 1969-73, in which the mean excess return for all funds was negative. CREF's return was approximately –4.9 percent per annum.

A possible explanation for these divergent results has been advanced by Dr. James L. Farrell, Jr., investment officer of the College Retirement Equities Fund. Referring to the 1957-68 period he stated:

> Stocks over this period earned approximately seven percentage points more than the risk-free investments. The combination of low interest rates and shrinking risk premiums provided one of the best bull market periods of all time. The expected bull market risk-reward relationship manifested itself quite clearly over this period.
>
> The overall period since 1968 can, however, be characterized as a fairly severe bear market for stocks. Risk-free rates (treasury bills) averaged something like 6%. The Standard and Poor's 500 stock index earned 2% per annum over the period. Stocks thus lost four percentage points per annum over this period. The bear market manifested itself quite clearly over the 1969-73 period.[57]

From the long and varied assemblage of different studies analyzed in this chapter, the inevitable conclusion is that, with rare exceptions, these pension funds are not outperforming the market when risk is taken into consideration. Moreover, these institutional funds are performing more poorly than an unmanaged portfolio with similar risk. Again, there are several exceptions, but these are probably due to chance occurrences.

This points to the fact that, in most cases, these funds would have performed better if they had followed a buy and hold strategy at a given risk level. Since other studies have also substantiated these findings, radical changes have begun in the management of equity portfolios. That is, the risk level desired has become the major decision for the portfolio manager, while the importance of turnover and trading has been definitely diminishing.

Table 3-20
Risk Adjusted Return, Beta Coefficient and Mean Excess Return for CREF, Standard and Poor's 500 Stock Index and Selected Mutual Funds

	1957-73			1957-68			1969-73		
	Mean Excess Return (Quarterly)	Beta	Performance Measure Alpha	Mean Excess Return (Quarterly)	Beta	Performance Measure Alpha	Mean Excess Return (Quarterly)	Beta	Performance Measure Alpha
G Chemical Fund	1.86	1.05	3.156	2.55	1.13	2.335	0.00	0.87	−3.48
G Diversified Growth Stock Fund	0.99	1.31	1.384	2.75	1.22	2.508	−3.50	1.35	−8.60
G Dreyfus Fund	1.72	1.07	2.514	3.13	1.04	5.320	−2.38	1.09	−5.16
G Keystone (K-2) Growth Fund	0.98	1.26	−1.220	2.27	1.25	0.380	−2.12	1.24	−3.52
G Mass. Investors Growth Stock Fund	1.48	1.16	1.187	2.19	1.17	0.616	−0.88	1.04	0.64
G National Investors Corp.	1.56	1.13	1.629	2.38	1.08	2.003	−0.88	1.11	0.92
G Price (T. Rowe) Growth Stock Fund	1.50	1.08	1.593	2.13	0.99	1.629	−1.05	1.11	0.24
G Technology Fund	1.38	1.13	0.909	2.42	1.13	1.815	−1.80	1.15	−2.60
G United Science	0.85	1.24	−1.659	2.00	1.24	−0.630	−2.60	1.14	−6.24
G Johnston Mutual Fund	1.43	0.97	1.762	2.12	0.89	2.285	−0.65	1.05	1.60
G Keystone (S-3) Growth Common	1.14	1.27	−0.621	2.15	1.22	0.108	−2.10	1.30	−3.20
G National Sec. Growth Stock Series	0.92	1.20	−1.216	2.32	1.14	1.345	−3.08	1.15	−7.72
IG Eaton & Howard Stock Fund	0.63	0.99	−1.519	1.55	0.94	−0.342	−1.85	1.04	−3.24
IG Fidelity Fund	1.19	1.00	0.680	2.00	1.01	0.970	−1.25	0.99	−1.04
IG Fundamental Investors	0.39	1.07	−2.805	1.59	1.07	−1.087	−2.48	1.04	−5.76
IG Investment Co. of America	1.45	1.03	1.597	2.43	0.99	2.829	−1.32	1.07	−1.00
IG Investors Stock Fund	0.67	1.05	−1.604	1.39	1.01	−1.469	−1.60	1.16	−1.76

IG	Massachusetts Investors Trust	0.84	0.97	–0.597	1.50	0.99	–0.890	–1.40	0.98	–1.68
IG	State Street Investment Corp.	1.37	1.02	1.318	2.25	0.92	2.596	–1.50	1.14	–1.44
IG	United Income	1.23	0.94	1.084	2.16	0.89	2.445	–1.35	0.96	–1.56
IG	Washington Mutual Investors Fund	0.79	0.85	–0.308	1.36	0.80	–0.128	–1.30	1.04	–1.04
IG	Affiliated Fund	1.39	0.89	1.928	2.25	0.84	3.153	–1.38	1.07	–1.24
IG	American Mutual Fund	1.15	0.93	0.805	1.94	0.89	1.565	–1.15	1.01	–0.56
IG	Broad Street Investing Corp.	1.05	0.89	0.568	1.60	0.86	0.414	–0.43	0.97	2.16
IG	Colonial Fund	0.90	0.88	0.009	1.75	0.85	1.084	–1.60	0.97	–2.52
IG	Dividend Shares	0.99	0.86	0.451	1.60	0.84	0.553	–0.85	0.91	0.24
IG	Group Sec. Common Stock Fund	0.99	0.87	0.410	1.80	0.91	0.866	–0.62	0.87	1.00
B	Axe-Houghton Fund B	0.69	0.88	–0.830	1.70	0.84	0.953	–2.10	0.84	–5.04
B	Boston Fund	0.49	0.68	–0.814	1.05	0.61	–0.045	–1.30	0.85	–1.80
B	Commonwealth Investment Co.	0.51	0.77	–1.101	1.11	0.72	–0.571	–1.40	0.83	–2.28
B	Eaton & Howard Balanced Fund	0.60	0.62	–0.129	1.10	0.58	0.363	–0.60	0.72	0.48
B	Investors Mutual	0.38	0.66	–1.172	0.92	0.61	–0.565	–1.17	0.78	–1.56
B	Loomis-Sayles Mutual Fund	0.75	0.68	0.225	1.23	0.60	0.744	–0.83	0.85	0.08
B	Massachusetts Fund	0.73	0.69	0.104	1.24	0.65	0.436	–0.83	0.82	–0.04
B	George Putnam Fund of Boston	1.05	0.78	1.017	1.56	0.77	0.880	–0.50	0.76	1.04
B	Scudder, Stevens & Clark Balanced Fund	0.32	0.80	–1.984	0.66	0.76	–2.649	–0.92	0.89	–0.12
B	Stein Roe & Farnham Balanced Fund	0.96	0.79	0.616	1.60	0.71	1.458	–0.97	0.91	–0.24
B	Wellington Fund	0.44	0.67	–0.973	0.87	0.62	–0.835	–1.28	0.79	–1.96
	College Retirement Equities Fund (CREF)	1.02	1.10	–0.400	1.72	1.05	–0.428	–1.22	1.13	–0.36
	Standard and Poor's 500 Stock Index	1.02	1.00	—						

Note: Code letters are G = growth fund; IG = income growth fund; B = balanced fund.

Source: College Retirement Equities Fund, New York, 1974.

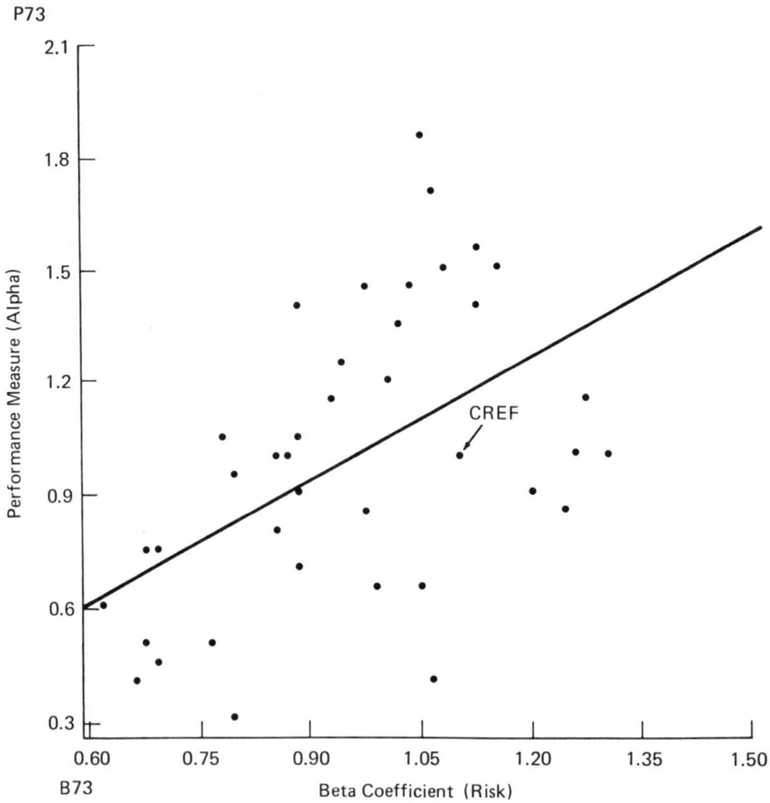

[a]Annualized alpha.

Figure 3-5. Performance Measure[a] and Beta for CREF, *Standard and Poor's* 500, and Mutual Fund Sample (1957-73). Source: Computed from data in Table 3-20.

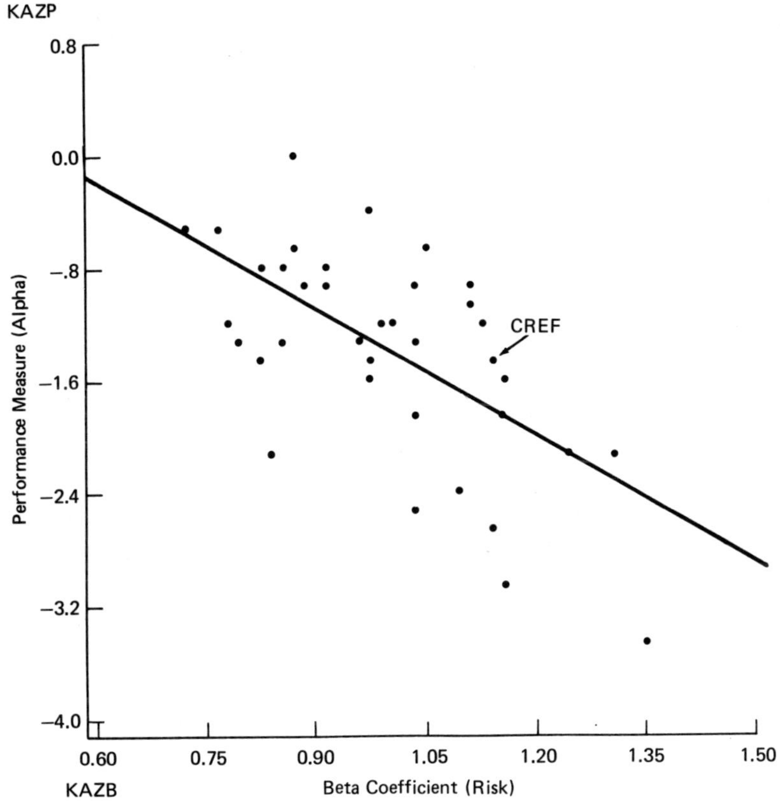

[a]Annualized alpha.

Figure 3-6. Performance Measure[a] and Beta for CREF, *Standard and Poor's* 500, and Mutual Fund Sample (1969-73). Source: Computed from data in Table 3-20.

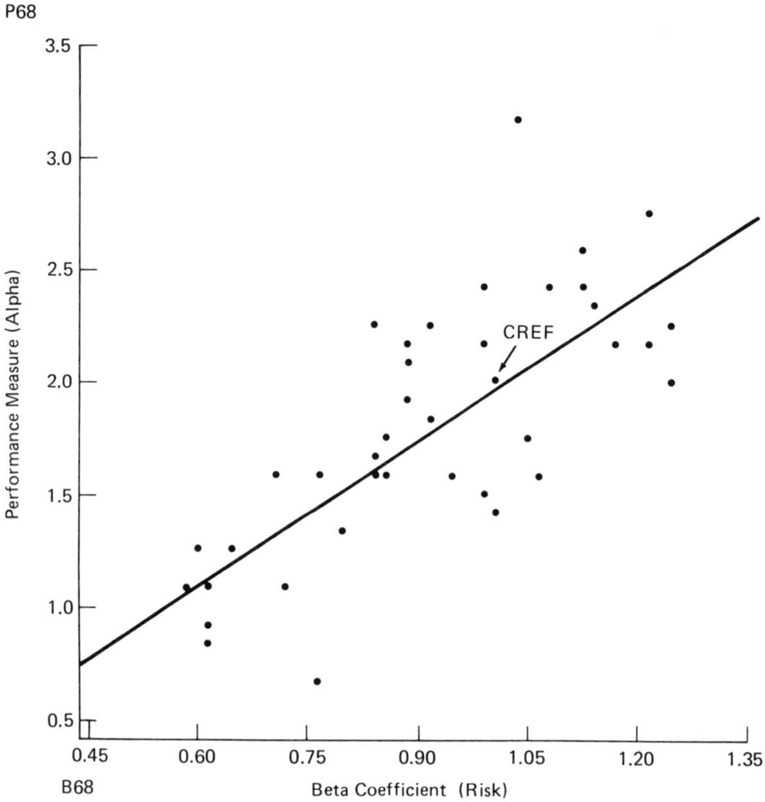

[a]Annualized alpha.

Figure 3-7. Performance Measure[a] and Beta for CREF, *Standard and Poor's* 500, and Mutual Fund Sample (1957-68). Source: Computed from data in Table 3-20.

4 Other Institutional Performance

The performance of private pension funds cannot be generalized to represent that of all institutional investors. Therefore, this chapter includes a review of some recent performance studies on mutual funds, insurance companies, and college endowments.

Table 4-1 presents a compilation of the compounded rates of return for the nine-year period ending December 31, 1973.[1] As can be seen, the best nine-year performance was for a portfolio consisting of 90-day treasury bills. This table includes performance results for bank-administered equity funds, insurance company separate equity accounts, and income equity mutual funds, among others. It presents a clear indication of the relative rates of return for the 1966-73 period.

Mutual Funds

There have certainly been many performance studies of mutual funds.[2] This being the case, it would be superfluous to discuss them in great detail. However, it is necessary to review the major studies in order to gain a better understanding of total institutional investor performance. The major emphasis is upon recent studies that employed the risk-adjusted performance measure.

It is generally acknowledged that mutual funds have no monopoly in their forecasting of security prices. As far back as 40 years ago, the Securities and Exchange Commission concluded that:

> The entire group of management investment companies proper failed to perform better than an index of leading common stocks and probably performed somewhat worse than the index over the 1927-1935 period.[3]

Thus, the mutual fund industry has been under close scrutiny for many, many years.

The conclusions reached in a more recent comprehensive Securi-

Table 4-1
Comparative Historical Performance Results, 1966-73[a]

	Cumulative Periods Through December 31, 1973					Equity Market Cycles		
	1 Year Since 1/1/73	3 Years Since 1/1/71	5 Years Since 1/1/69	7 Years Since 1/1/67	9 Years Since 1/1/65	1/1/69 Through 12/31/72	1/1/66 Through 12/31/68	1/1/66 Through 12/31/72
S & P 500 Stock Index	–14.72	5.08	2.00	6.17	4.89	6.66	7.37	6.96
New York Stock Exchange Index	–17.12	4.06	0.53	5.65	4.61	5.50	8.94	6.96
Dow Jones Industrial Average	–13.36	4.11	1.67	4.91	3.36	5.82	2.95	4.58
90-day treasury bill portfolio	7.00	5.12	5.69	5.45	5.20	5.37	4.81	5.13
26 insurance company separate equity funds	–19.54	2.24	–0.44	3.69	3.44	5.38	7.70	5.85
20 major bank commingled equity funds	–20.75	3.96	0.24	4.65	3.99	6.29	8.00	6.95
Income equity mutual funds	–16.03	2.54	–0.63	5.18	4.94	3.62	10.10	6.59

[a]Time weighted rates of return including dividends.

Source: *1974 Investment Performance Survey*, Dreher, Rogers & Associates, Inc., 1974, p. 4.

ties and Exchange Commission (SEC) study were not significantly different from the above-mentioned study.[4] The analysis ended with this now-familar theme:

> The average performance by the (mutual) funds did not differ appreciably from what would have been achieved by an unmanaged portfolio with the same division among asset types.[5]

This conclusion is consistent with prior findings that investment companies lack superior predictive abilities.

Irwin Friend, Marshall Blume, and Jean Crockett studied mutual funds over the 1960-69 period.[6] Although they employed sophisticated measurement techniques, their conclusions did not differ appreciably from other earlier studies.

In a rather comprehensive study of 115 mutual funds, Michael C. Jensen found that their performance for the 20-year period from 1945 to 1964 was no better than an unmanaged portfolio of similar risk.[7] The mean performance measure, alpha, was −1.1 percent, that is, these funds earned, on average, 1.1 percent less per year (compounded continuously) than an unmanaged portfolio with a similar risk level.

Table 4-2 presents Jensen's findings. Only 39 of the 115 funds had positive alphas during the study period, and Jensen comments that:

> . . . (these) funds are not able to forecast future security prices well enough to recover their research expenses, management fees and commission expenses.[8]

These mutual funds were highly diversified, having a mean coefficient of determination (R^2) of 0.87. This signifies that 87 percent of the movements in these funds can be explained by movements in the market. The mean beta coefficient is 0.84. Jensen concludes:

> It seems clear . . . that there is little evidence that any of these 115 mutual funds . . . possessed substantial forecasting ability.[9]

The most recent SEC study analyzed the performance of 125 mutual funds over the 10-year period from 1960 to 1969.[10] Using risk and return to analyze performance, the study surprisingly concluded that, for the entire 10-year period, these mutual funds did slightly better than an unmanaged portfolio with similar risk. However, for the intraperiod from 1960 to 1964, the reverse was found.

Table 4-2
Jensen's Performance Results 1945-64

	Mean	Median	Range	
			Minimum	Maximum
Alpha[a]	−1.1%	−0.9%	−8.0%	5.8%
Beta	0.84	0.85	0.22	1.41
Diversification measure (R^2)	0.87	0.90	0.45	0.98

[a]Annualized.

Source: Jensen, Michael, "The Performance of Mutual Funds in the Period 1945-1964," *Journal of Finance*, May 1968, pp. 389-419.

One possible explanation for this apparent discrepancy may be that the level of diversification of these mutual funds was relatively low—an R^2 of 0.60, that is, only 60 percent of the variation in the monthly fund returns can be explained by movements in the market. However, the methodology employed assumes a high degree of diversification. Perhaps this fact explains the varied performance results found by this SEC study.

Another important finding was the negative relationship between portfolio turnover and performance.[11] This revealed that, on average, a 10 percent increase in the turnover rate would have reduced mutual fund performance by approximately 0.6 percent per year. For example, with a \$500 million fund this 10 percent increase in turnover would have cost approximately \$3 million per year. This discovery points out how mutual funds failed to use trading to increase returns. It further implies that performance could have been increased merely by reducing turnover.

One of the leaders in the mutual fund performance field is Wiesenberger Services. This firm publishes the informative *Mutual Fund Performance Monthly*, which analyzes the following variables each month: performance, risk, rate of return, objectives, and size.[12] Table 4-3 presents these variables for the period from January 1, 1964 to December 31, 1973.

Each mutual fund has a stated objective that should indicate the types of investments and risks the fund is willing to assume. In recognition of this fact, Table 4-3 shows the mean returns of the mutual funds, classified by objective.

As would be expected, there is a strong relationship between the stated objective of a fund and its risk level (beta). For example, those

Table 4-3
Mutual Fund Performance Ranked by Fund Objective[a]

	January 1, 1966 to December 31, 1973					
	10 Years 1/1/66 to 12/31/73			5 Years 1/1/69 to 12/31/73		
Objective	Alpha[c]	Beta	Adjusted[b] Change In Net Asset Value (%)	Alpha[c]	Beta	Adjusted[b] Change In Net Asset Value (%)
Standard and Poor's 500 Stock Index		1.00	+69.60		1.00	+9.01
Maximum capital gain	−1.17%	1.32	+79.37	−11.4%	1.33	−36.41
Long term growth and income	−.98%	1.08	+65.40	−5.54%	1.09	−13.54
Growth	−.28%	1.06	+75.62	−4.3%	1.09	−9.98
Growth and current income	−.84%	1.01	+62.30	−3.8%	1.03	−8.61
Growth and income plus stability	+.44%	0.95	+74.34	−3.5%	0.99	−6.99
Income and growth	+1.76%	0.88	+84.65	−2.2%	0.87	−3.68
Income, growth and stability	+.16%	0.90	+63.74	−1.78%	0.92	−0.40
Income stability and growth	+1.23%	0.73	+66.71	−1.12%	0.73	+0.96
Income	+1.73%	0.71	+69.08	−1.6%	0.69	−2.29
Stability, income and growth	+0.04%	0.77	+53.31	−1.22%	0.81	+2.19

[a]The arithmetic mean performance.

[b]Change in net asset value for period, with distribution from realized capital gains reinvested and income dividends added back.

[c]Mean annual alpha.

Source: Wiesenberger Services, Inc., *Mutual Fund Performance Monthly*, New York, January 1974.

funds with an objective of maximum capital gains had the highest beta coefficient, 1.32. During the 10-year period, the highest risk category demonstrated inferior performance on a risk-adjusted basis. This does not indicate that the actual rate of return was inferior to that of the market. On the contrary, this fund group had a greater rate of return (appreciation and dividends included) than did the Standard and Poor's 500 Stock Index. However, this superiority did not sufficiently compensate for the higher risk taken.

The two mutual fund categories that had the lowest risk levels both outperformed the market on a risk-adjusted basis. This was achieved even though the income group did not attain a greater rate of return than the market. However, because of the lower risk level taken by this group, the return on a risk-adjusted basis was superior to that of the market.

The results differ noticeably, however, during the five-year period. All fund groups had a negative risk-adjusted performance for this time span. In fact, the high-risk mutual fund group had a –11.4 percent alpha. Moreover, while the market increased 9 percent, the group of high-risk mutuals decreased over 36 percent. Even the low-risk income group had a negative risk-adjusted performance. Giving equal weight to each group, the mean annual alpha was –7.3 percent for all mutual funds studied during the five-year period, with a mean beta coefficient of 0.96. The mean return for all funds was –7.88 percent while the Standard and Poor's 500 Stock Index advanced 9.01 percent.[13]

These mutual funds are in good company. For the 1969-1973 period, almost all institutional investors studied showed poor equity performance when risk is considered.[14]

Table 4-4 summarizes the performance of mutual funds as ranked by their asset size.[15] The largest size category represents, in dollars, over 50 percent of the mutual fund industry.

Some surprising results can be found in this table. There seems to be a positive relationship between size and performance. However, this is not consistent for all periods. Also, there is an apparent weak inverse relationship between size and risk (beta). Interestingly enough, the largest funds had the best performance for both periods. This is true whether or not risk is considered.

Giving equal weight to each group, the mean alpha for all mutual funds during the five-year period was –6.16 percent. These funds assumed higher risk levels over the five-year period than they had during the entire 10-year period.

Table 4-4
Mutual Funds' Performance[a] Ranked by Size

	10 Years			5 Years		
Size	Alpha	Beta	% Change In Net Asset Value	Alpha	Beta	% Change In Net Asset Value
$300 million and over	+0.96%	1.03	+93.28	−2.46	1.03	−2.49
Standard and Poor's 500		1.00	+69.60		1.00	+9.01
$200-$300 million	+0.61%	1.01	+80.39	−3.24	1.05	−7.10
$100-$200 million	+0.60	1.00	+79.57	−3.26	1.03	−6.24
$50-$100 million	+0.34	1.01	+75.57	−5.6	1.09	−15.42
$25-$50 million	−0.43	0.98	+63.15	−6.36	1.12	−18.09
$10-$25 million	−1.58	1.02	+49.04	−7.64	1.08	−23.13
$5-$10 million	−0.53	1.02	+66.52	−8.62	1.17	−26.52
$1-$5 million	−3.46	1.11	+29.50	−12.10	1.22	−36.72
Average of all funds	−0.44	1.02	+57.68	−6.16	1.10	−16.96

[a]Arithmetic mean performance.
Source: Wiesenberger Services, Inc., *Mutual Fund Performance Monthly*, January 1974.

Notwithstanding their stated objectives, it seems clear that most mutual funds cannot outperform the market on a risk-adjusted basis. Moreover, they generally underperform the market. The notion of superior performance on the part of mutual funds is unfounded. Their major purpose and selling point should be their ability to provide the individual with an opportunity to invest in a fully diversified portfolio with as small an amount as $1,000. Without this diversification, the investor takes added risk that is not compensated by the market. The sooner mutual funds realize that diversification, not superior performance, is their main selling point, the healthier this once-dynamic industry will become.

Life Insurance Companies

The life insurance industry has been rather restrained in its equity investing, mainly because of statutory restrictions. In fact, in New York State these companies are limited to investing a maximum of 10 percent of their total assets in common stock.[16] This is of particular importance since the largest life insurance companies are located there. In 1973 all life insurance companies held over $19 billion in common equities.[17] Table 4-5 presents their assets for 1972 and 1973 and is categorized by asset types. Table 4-6 traces the significant changes in their common stock investing during the 1917-73 period.

In order to better compete for pension accounts, especially against bank trust departments, life insurance companies introduced separate fund accounts in the early 1960s. These accounts are held separately from all other assets of the life company. This is because state laws allow the separate accounts to be invested without the usual investment restrictions. Table 4-7 summarizes the assets of these accounts. In 1973 common stocks represented over 75 percent of the $10 billion in these funds. Such accounts are assumed to be particularly attractive to pension funds since the rates of return are variable and theoretically have no upper limit. Obviously, the lure of these funds is the expectation of better investment performance.

The Securities and Exchange Commission's *Institutional Investor Study* analyzed 200 separate insurance accounts over the five-year period from 1965 to 1969.[18] Table 4-8 demonstrates that there is a high positive relationship between risk and risk-adjusted performance. The SEC has observed a similar relationship in other institutional investors.[19] The results in Table 4-9 show that on a risk-adjusted basis, these funds did slightly better than an unmanaged portfolio with similar risk. Interpreting the favorable performance results, the SEC cautions the reader against generalizing these findings.[20] It advises that this time period may, indeed, be a unique one. Notwithstanding these cautions, the results are impressive in contrast with the other institutional performance studies discussed. However, the five-year period may be too brief to satisfactorily measure long-term performance.

Table 4-10 presents different results for a more extensive period. It shows that insurance company separate accounts had an average annual compounded rate of return of 3.09 percent for the 10-year period ending June 30, 1974.[21] For this same period, both the Standard and Poor's 500 Stock Index and the Dow Jones Industrial Average outperformed these funds. Moreover, for all periods studied, these insurance company funds did more poorly than the market. The mean beta coefficient was 1.08 for the five-year period ending June 30, 1974. This was a slightly higher risk level than that of the market.[22] On a risk-adjusted basis, these accounts also proved to be inferior performers.

In summation, it is found that the results for life insurance company separate accounts generally prove to be conflicting. During the 1965-69 period, positive risk-adjusted performance was found while for the later period, 1969-74, an inferior investment performance was demonstrated. Furthermore, for the 10-year period from 1965 to 1974, the annual time-weighted rate of return for these accounts was significantly inferior to the market return.

A frequently overlooked institutional investor is the property-liability insurance company. As of the end of 1973 these funds had total assets in excess of $60 billion.[23] In a recent study of 20 of these insurance companies, Gary Schlarbaum found that, for the 1958-67 period, their equity performance was inferior to an unmanaged portfolio of similar risk.[24] These 20 companies represented over one-third of the total assets in this industry.

During the 10-year study period these property-liability insurance companies had a mean compounded annual rate of return that was 11.61 percent. This compares unfavorably with the Standard and Poor's 500 return of 12.08 percent and with the 15.14 percent achieved by equal weights of all New York Stock Exchange (NYSE)-listed stocks.[25] An equally weighted random portfolio with similar risk returned 14.21 percent during this period. The study concluded that:

> The returns earned by the insurance company portfolios were significantly lower than those earned by random portfolios of equivalent risk regardless of the risk measure used. This means that the performance of the (property-liability) insurance company portfolios was unambiguously inferior to the performance of randomly selected portfolios over the period 1958-1967.[26]

The poor performance of these insurance companies was even more significant given the fact that their returns were calculated on a gross basis while most mutual fund studies utilize the net return basis (after management fees).[27] Schlarbaum explains the impact which these findings have on both the industry and the consumer:

> The implication is that insurance regulators should carefully examine investment performance in evaluating requests for higher insurance rates. The buyer of insurance coverage should not have to pay higher rates because the investment portfolios of the companies have earned below-average returns.[28]

Educational Endowments Comparisons

The investment management activities of nonprofit organizations are a segment of the institutional investment market that is rarely

Table 4-5
Acquisitions and Change in Holdings of Investments, United States Life Insurance Companies (in Millions of Dollars)

Type of Investment	1972 Acquired in Year	1972 Held at Year End	1972 Change in Holdings in Year	1973 Acquired in Year	1973 Held at Year End	1973 Change in Holdings in Year
Government Securities						
Short term: 1 year or less						
U.S. treasury	$ 6,113	$ 338	$ +173	$ 5,317	$ 262	$ −76
U.S. federal agency	1,245	20	+3	1,536	36	+16
Foreign government and international agency	27	3	+2	52	5	+2
	7,385	361	+178	6,905	303	−58
Other: over 1 year						
U.S. treasury	488	3,489	−174	229	3,182	−307
U.S. federal agency	190	715	+105	239	848	+133
U.S. state and local	436	3,367	+4	501	3,412	+45
Foreign government and international agency	490	3,440	+259	416	3,658	+218
	1,604	11,011	+194	1,385	11,100	+89
Total government securities	8,989	11,372	+372	8,290	11,403	+31
Corporate securities						
Bonds, debentures, and notes						

Short term: 1 year or less	53,983	2,981	+211	74,318	3,004	+23
Other: over 1 year						
U.S.	13,640	78,478	+6,433	12,298	83,974	+5,496
Foreign	617	4,681	+298	443	4,818	+137
	68,240	86,140	+6,942	87,059	91,796	+5,656
Stocks						
Common	6,912	21,793	+5,014	6,492	19,606	–2,187
Preferred	1,556	5,052	+1,224	1,706	6,313	+1,261
	8,468	26,845	+6,238	8,198	25,919	–926
Total corporate securities	76,708	112,985	+13,180	95,257	117,715	+4,730
Mortgages						
Farm	700	5,678	+77	1,006	5,996	+318
Nonfarm						
F.H.A.	331	9,962	–805	281	9,208	–754
N.H.A.	19	550	–19	21	532	–18
V.A.	182	4,660	–344	237	4,402	–258
Conventional	7,464	56,098	+2,543	9,918	61,231	+5,133
Total mortgages	8,696	76,948	+1,452	11,463	81,369	+4,421
Real estate	976	7,295	+391	1,177	7,693	+398
Policy loans	3,252	18,003	+938	4,602	20,199	+2,196
Cash	xxx	1,981	+218	xxx	2,071	+90
Other assets	xxx	11,146	+1,077	xxx	11,986	+840
Total assets	$98,621	$239,730	$+17,628	$120,789	$252,436	$+12,706

Source: *Life Insurance Fact Book 1974*, The Institute of Life Insurance, New York, p. 73.

Table 4-6
Corporate Securities Owned by United States Life Insurance Companies (in Millions of Dollars)

	Bonds				Stocks					
Year	United States	Foreign	Total	% of Assets	Common	Preferred	Total	% of Assets	Total Amount	% of Assets
1917	a	a	$ 1,975	33.2	a	a	$ 83	1.4	$ 2,058	34.6
1920	a	a	1,949	26.7	a	a	75	1.0	2,024	27.7
1925	a	a	3,022	26.2	a	a	81	0.7	3,103	26.9
1930	a	a	4,929	26.0	a	a	519	2.8	5,448	28.8
1935	a	a	5,314	22.9	a	a	583	2.5	5,897	25.4
1940	a	a	8,645	28.1	a	a	605	2.0	9,250	30.1
1945	a	a	10,060	22.5	a	a	999	2.2	11,059	24.7
1946	a	a	11,775	24.5	a	a	1,249	2.6	13,024	27.1
1947	$14,329	$ 382	14,711	28.4	$ 357	$1,033	1,390	2.7	16,101	31.1
1948	18,388	456	18,844	33.9	373	1,055	1,428	2.6	20,272	36.5
1949	20,893	513	21,406	35.9	460	1,258	1,718	2.9	23,124	38.8
1950	22,607	641	23,248	36.3	649	1,454	2,103	3.3	25,351	39.6
1951	25,147	743	25,890	37.9	820	1,401	2,221	3.3	28,111	41.2
1952	28,164	905	29,069	39.6	963	1,483	2,446	3.3	31,515	42.9
1953	30,750	1,115	31,865	40.6	1,042	1,531	2,573	3.3	34,438	43.9
1954	32,774	1,258	34,032	40.3	1,536	1,732	3,268	3.9	37,300	44.2

1955	34,629	1,283	35,912	39.7	1,889	1,744	3,633	4.0	39,545	43.7
1956	36,606	1,434	38,040	39.6	1,952	1,551	3,503	3.7	41,543	43.3
1957	39,065	1,600	40,665	40.1	1,867	1,524	3,391	3.3	44,056	43.4
1958	41,234	1,764	42,998	40.0	2,548	1,561	4,109	3.8	47,107	43.8
1959	43,142	1,884	45,026	39.6	2,954	1,607	4,561	4.0	49,587	43.6
1960	44,709	2,031	46,740	39.1	3,183	1,798	4,981	4.2	51,721	43.3
1961	46,595	2,292	48,887	38.5	4,223	2,035	6,258	4.9	55,145	43.4
1962	48,522	2,602	51,124	38.4	4,119	2,183	6,302	4.7	57,426	43.1
1963	50,620	2,833	53,453	37.9	4,820	2,315	7,135	5.0	60,588	42.9
1964	52,408	3,046	55,454	37.1	5,422	2,516	7,938	5.3	63,392	42.4
1965	54,835	3,409	58,244	36.7	6,263	2,863	9,126	5.7	67,370	42.4
1966	57,105	3,714	60,819	36.3	6,003	2,829	8,832	5.3	69,651	41.6
1967	60,835	3,852	64,687	36.4	7,810	3,067	10,877	6.1	75,564	42.5
1968	64,396	3,914	68,310	36.2	9,995	3,235	13,230	7.0	81,540	43.2
1969	66,813	4,046	70,859	36.0	10,318	3,389	13,707	6.9	84,566	42.9
1970	68,711	4,387	73,098	35.3	11,873	3,547	15,420	7.4	88,518	42.7
1971	74,699	4,499	79,198	35.7	16,779	3,828	20,607	9.3	99,805	45.0
1972	81,244	4,896	86,140	35.9	21,793	5,052	26,845	11.2	112,985	47.1
1973	86,848	4,948	91,796	36.4	19,606	6,313	25,919	10.3	117,715	46.7

[a]Not available.

Source: *Life Insurance Fact Book 1974*, The Institute of Life Insurance, New York, p. 77.

Table 4-7
Distribution of Assets Held in Separate Accounts of United States Life Insurance Companies (in Millions of Dollars)

	Amount							
		Stocks						
Year	Bonds	Common	Preferred	Mortgages	Real Estate	Cash	Other	Total
1967	$ 114	$1,055	$ 9	$ 14	a	$13	$ 2	$ 1,207
1968	233	1,915	31	20	$ 1	48	21	2,269
1969	638	2,745	48	36	1	52	99	3,619
1970	878	3,955	86	37	2	69	34	5,061
1971	763	6,416	83	87	24	88	62	7,523
1972	948	8,673	71	120	96	68	82	10,058
1973	1,581	7,900	53	171	186	64	75	10,030
	Percent							
1967	10%	87%	1%	1%	b	1%	b	100%
1968	10	85	1	1	b	2	1%	100
1969	18	76	1	1	b	1	3	100
1970	17	78	2	1	b	1	1	100
1971	10	85	1	1	1%	1	1	100
1972	9	86	1	1	1	1	1	100
1973	16	79	b	2	2	b	1	100

[a]Less than $500,000.

[b]Less than 0.5 percent.

Source: *Life Insurance Fact Book 1974*, The Institute of Life Insurance, New York, p. 85.

Table 4-8
Regression Coefficient Results for Describing the Relationship Between Insurance Company Separate Account Performance and Account Characteristics

Independent Variable	Dependent Variable: Performance (Alpha) Regression Coefficient	Performance (Alpha) *t* Value	Turnover Regression Coefficient	Turnover *t* Value
Performance (alpha)			8.05	0.56
Turnover rate	0.00053	0.56		
Volatility (beta)	0.92	5.30	0.90	0.04
Account common stock holdings	–0.00023	–0.50	–0.056	0.99
Total assets of managing insurer	0.0000090	1.94	–0.00031	0.52
Diversification measure (R^2)	81	–4.23	22.19	0.85
	$\bar{R}^2$ = .025		$\bar{R}^2$ = 0	

Source: Securities and Exchange Commission, *Institutional Investor Study*, vol. II (Washington, D.C.: U.S. Government Printing Office, 1971), p. 745.

sufficiently analyzed.[29] This is unfortunate in view of their significant size, rapid growth rate, and serious portfolio problems. The combination of historically conservative investment policies, inflationary pressures, and accelerating demands for greater investment income has placed these institutions in a particularly difficult position. The need for income to support their programs has been especially acute in recent years.

A recent critical study found that educational endowment performance was "not good."[30] Partly in response to this, many endowment trustees are now pursuing investment objectives (in terms of total return) as aggressive as those of pension and mutual funds. Moreover, in response to critics who feel that they have an overly conservative approach to investments, many nonprofit institutions are splitting the management of their portfolio assets in order to encourage competition between managers. In fact, one leading university employs eight different managers for its \$175 million endowment fund, and it seeks a minimum average return of 12 percent per annum.[31]

The two most important categories of nonprofit portfolios are college and university endowment funds and private foundations.

Table 4-9
Summary of Investment Return Data for the Separate Accounts Classified by Volatility

Volatility Range	Number of Accounts	Average Number of Observations per Account	Monthly Account Return Percent per Month	Monthly Market Return Percent per Month	Performance Measure (Alpha) Percent per Month	Volatility Measure (Average Beta)	Portfolio Turnover (1969)	Account Size (Average Common Stock Holdings) $ Millions	Advisor Size (Average Assets) $ Billions
0.0-0.4	3	40.7	0.53	0.46	–0.09	0.20	75.4	1.3	2.0
0.4-0.8	13	41.3	0.32	0.22	–0.06	0.64	43.7	23.2	14.8
0.8-1.0	30	48.1	0.42	0.31	0.08	0.93	34.9	11.1	5.5
1.0-1.2	24	52.0	0.54	0.40	0.16	1.08	60.4	48.7	4.2
over 1.2	10	27.1	0.36	0.25	0.30	1.36	64.8	2.9	2.8
Total	80	45.3	0.44	0.32	0.10	0.95	49.2	23.0	6.2

Note: All averages are unweighted.

Source: Securities and Exchange Commission, *Institutional Investor Study*, Vol. II (Washington, D.C.: U.S. Government Printing Office, 1971).

Table 4-10
Time-weighted Rates of Return, Cumulative Periods Ending June 30, 1974

	1 Year	3 Years	5 Years	7 Years	10 Years
Standard and Poor's 500	(14.54)	(1.79)	0.71	2.48	3.77
Dow Jones Industrials	(6.12)	0.22	2.13	2.76	3.35
Bank-pooled equity funds–I	(15.34)%	(3.68)%	0.15%	1.48%	3.30%
Bank-pooled equity funds–II	(14.42)	(3.80)	0.89	2.73	3.63
Insurance company separate accounts	(13.84)	(5.19)	(1.31)	0.54	3.09
Growth and income mutual funds	(11.28)	(4.13)	(0.84)	1.36	3.82
Growth mutual funds	(14.81)	(8.19)	(3.47)	(1.71)	3.93
Inv. counselor equity portfolio	(8.56)	(1.30)	1.27	—	—

Source: Callan Associates, Inc., San Francisco, California, 1974.

However, this analysis is limited to the educational endowment funds.

Rates of Return

A college or university endowment is a perpetual fund whose investment income usually supplements operating revenues of the school.[32] Increases in educational expenses have generally outpaced the growth of endowment assets or returns. In fact, in 1970 it was estimated that these educational endowment funds returned roughly 4 percent, which was as low as government bond rates at that time.[33] This low return has contributed both to the curtailment of many college services and to increased tuition.

As of 1972 it was estimated that total endowment funds were at $15 billion, or slightly less than one-half the size of all mutual fund assets.[34] In fact the largest 10 universities account for over $5 billion, or 35 percent of total endowment assets.

As mentioned earlier, educational endowments are becoming quite aggressive in their investment portfolios. As of mid-year 1972, over 65 percent of the assets of the 35 university endowments surveyed were in common stock.[35] In fact in 1973 Princeton University had 81 percent of its portfolio in common stock, while the University of Chicago had over 75 percent in equities.[36] The University of

Rochester, one of the most aggressive endowments, earned a –21.7 percent return on its portfolio for 1973.[37] This compares with a Standard and Poor's 500 Stock Index return of –14 percent.

A recent Ford Foundation study admonished most endowments for being overly conservative with their investing.[38] Table 4-11 presents the rate of return earned by 15 educational endowments. The average annual return over the 10-year period 1959-68 was 8.7 percent. This compares with 9.2 percent and 14.6 percent for balanced and growth mutual funds, respectively.[39] Furthermore, the study blames their highly conservative investment philosophy for this relatively poor performance. This report maintains that the endowment funds should emphasize the maximization of total long-term income rather than continue their present approach of maximizing current income.[40] The 15 educational endowments studied had sharply lower returns than did the more aggressive University of Rochester fund. However, this analysis failed to recognize the higher risk level that the University of Rochester was willing to accept. Also, this 10-year period from 1959 to 1968 was probably one of the best decades for the stock market in modern history.

Table 4-12 traces the performance of these educational endowments over the 13-year period ending June 30, 1971. The average annual compounded return for these funds was 7.93 percent.[41] The returns were 6.94 percent for the five-year period and 6.70 percent for the 10-year span. For the three separate time periods, the University of Rochester earned 11.59 percent, 10.51 percent, and 5.88 percent, respectively.[42] There is a wide range of differences in fund performance results. Fund # 1, for instance, achieved consist-

Table 4-11
Total Return Comparisons of Educational Funds Versus Mutual Funds, 1959-68

	Cumulative	Annual Average
Fifteen educational institutions – average	134%	8.7%
Twenty-one balanced funds – average	143	9.2
The University of Rochester	283	14.4
Ten large general growth funds – average	295	14.6

Note: Total return includes both (a) appreciation and (b) interest and dividends, which are assumed to have been reinvested.

Source: Ford Foundation Study, *Managing Educational Endowments*, New York, July 1972, p. 3.

Table 4-12
Investment Performance of College Endowments, Mutual Funds, and Standard and Poor's 500 Stock Index

	Annual Average Total Return		
	Thirteen Years to June 30, 1971	Ten Years to June 30, 1971	Five Years to June 30, 1971
1. Twelve Educational Institutions			
1	11.94%	10.61%	12.73%
2	10.34	8.97	9.72
3	9.49	8.64	9.84
4	7.28	5.84	4.50
5	7.95%	7.00%	7.82%
6	7.61	6.03	7.26
7	7.43	6.35	6.11
8	6.97	5.88	5.58
9	7.06%	5.72%	5.84%
10	5.91	4.44	3.28
11	6.58	5.53	5.10
12	6.54	5.40	5.50
Average	7.93%	6.70%	6.94%
2. The University of Rochester	11.59%	10.51%	5.88%
3. Mean return of 21 balanced funds	7.50%	6.20%	5.64%
4. Standard and Poor's Index of 500 common stocks	9.83%	7.94%	6.81%

Note: The institutions are the same ones for which rates of return for years ending June 30, 1968, were tabulated in Appendix A-1 of the first (1969) edition of *Managing Educational Endowments.*

Total return includes both (a) appreciation, and (b) interest and dividends, which are assumed to have been reinvested. The unit method is used in calculating total return. The annual average return is on a compound basis.

Source: Ford Foundation Study, *Managing Educational Endowments*, July, 1972, p. 57-58.

ently higher rates of return, even during the latest five-year period when the stock market performed poorly. Interestingly, these college endowment funds outperformed balanced mutual funds for all periods studied.

In conclusion, it can only be shown that these 15 funds, on average, did not perform as well as other more aggressive funds such as growth mutuals. However, they did outperform the more conservative balanced mutual funds. Unfortunately, it is impossible to fully analyze the true performance of these endowment funds, since the Ford Foundation study did not take risk-level into account. All that can be safely said at this juncture is that these educational endowments generally performed more poorly than did the stock market over the 13-year period ending June 30, 1971.

In a more thorough performance study, J. Peter Williamson measured the returns of 36 educational endowments.[43] Table 4-13 compares the geometric annual rate of return for these funds with the Standard and Poor's 500 Stock Index. During the 10-year period ending June 30, 1971, these 36 endowments received a 6.05 percent mean return. This is in contrast to the market return of 7.94 percent over the same period. For the separate three- and five-year periods, both ending June 30, 1971, these endowments had returns of 4.70 percent and 6.06 percent, respectively. This compares favorably with the stock market return of 3.54 percent and 6.81 percent for the same two periods, respectively.

Risk Factors

At first glance, it seems that these endowment funds did not perform very well during the 10-year period when compared with the Standard and Poor's composite index. However, the risk level has not yet been considered, and a much more favorable picture will emerge when this is done. Table 4-14 indicates that the mean risk level (beta) for these funds is 0.63, that is, these endowment portfolios have approximately 35 percent less risk than the market. Given this risk level, the appropriate comparison portfolio is not the Standard and Poor's 500. With a beta of 0.63, an unmanaged portfolio of similar risk would have returned approximately 5.0 percent during this 10-year period. In other words, these education endowment funds were superior performers when risk is considered. This is true in spite of the market return of 7.94 percent.

The main criticism advanced by the two studies on educational endowment funds is only partially valid.[44] It is correct to say, judging from their risk level, that these funds are, indeed, conservative investors.[45] However, from the information available, it seems evident that these endowment funds compared quite favorably on a risk-adjusted performance basis. The fact that they have a great aversion to risk may be justified by the nature of their needs and functions.

Table 4-13
Educational Endowment Fund Rates of Return

	Period Ending June 30, 1971 Geometric Avg. Total Annual Return in %		
Fund	10 Years	5 Years	3 Years
1	10.61	12.73	8.40
2	8.97	9.72	6.72
3	8.64	9.84	5.60
4	7.99	11.24	8.14
5 (Standard and Poor's 500 Stock Index)	7.94	6.81	3.54
6	7.43	9.82	13.37
7	7.00	7.82	5.07
8	6.84	6.99	4.74
9	6.71	6.42	3.06
10	6.71	6.68	4.09
11	6.56	6.13	3.86
12	6.51	6.40	4.49
13	6.35	6.11	5.41
14	6.26	4.83	6.11
15	6.24	6.64	3.80
16	6.10	5.26	3.16
17	6.09	6.09	5.93
18	6.03	7.26	5.73
19	5.96	5.51	3.62
20	5.90	5.62	3.71
21	5.84	4.50	0.42
22	5.59	5.70	3.95
23	5.53	5.10	5.69
24	5.48	5.22	4.65
25	5.47	4.74	4.14
26	5.40	5.50	2.67
27	5.34	6.04	12.30
28	5.31	5.33	4.60
29	5.22	5.81	3.92
30	4.96	2.27	0.11
31	4.94	4.55	1.98
32	4.75	3.74	4.68
33	4.72	4.29	2.90
34	4.29	4.83	4.83
35	4.24	2.21	1.11
36	4.13	3.89	3.95
37	3.53	3.23	1.86
Mean return for 36 endowment funds	6.05	6.06	4.70

Note: Return includes appreciation, dividends, and interest.

Source: Williamson, J. Peter, *Performance Measurement and Investment Objectives For Educational Endowment Funds*, The Common Fund, New York, 1972, p. 28.

Table 4-14
Performance of 36 Educational Endowment Funds, 10 Years Ending June 30, 1971

Endowment Fund (1)	Beta Coefficient (2)	Correlation Coefficient of Characteristic Line (3)	Arithmetic Average Rate of Return (4)	Standard Deviation in Rate of Return (5)
1	0.83	0.942	11.60%	16.55%
2	0.24	0.848	6.35	5.30
3	0.78	0.986	9.82	15.00
4	0.64	0.936	8.60	12.81
5	0.85	0.967	9.69	16.57
6	0.58	0.962	7.48	11.28
7	0.41	0.875	6.33	8.86
8	0.69	0.959	7.56	13.66
9	0.65	0.980	7.34	12.61
10	1.14	0.806	9.41	26.65
11	0.69	0.925	7.37	14.04
12	0.36	0.550	5.98	12.48
13	0.66	0.968	7.16	12.88
14	0.89	0.985	7.94	17.12
15	0.68	0.984	7.01	13.01
16	0.66	0.989	6.89	12.63
17	0.72	0.914	7.03	14.95
18	0.63	0.988	6.69	12.05
19	0.66	0.980	6.62	12.65
20	0.67	0.962	6.58	13.09
21	0.80	0.965	6.90	15.63
22	0.48	0.852	5.87	10.71
23	0.54	0.929	5.95	10.88
24	0.65	0.978	6.25	12.60
25	0.66	0.957	6.21	13.08
26	0.82	0.962	6.53	16.15
27	0.47	0.950	5.58	9.27
28	0.63	0.977	5.92	12.18
29	0.54	0.813	5.67	12.43
30	8.43	0.943	5.26	8.69
31	0.69	0.942	5.54	13.89
32	0.36	0.820	5.04	8.27
33	0.63	0.940	4.93	12.60
34	0.58	0.955	4.82	11.38
35	0.52	0.946	4.59	10.28
36	0.48	0.954	3.95	9.44
Average	0.63	0.930	6.74	12.824

Source: Williamson, Peter, *Performance Measurement and Investment Objectives for Educational Endowment Funds*, The Common Fund, New York, 1972, p. 40.

What is needed is much more research into educational endowment performance. Extensive research must also be done on the portfolio performance and practices of private foundations, since no significant study of this type has, as of yet, been conducted.[46]

The concluding chapter discusses some of the implication of these institutional investor performance studies. Of particular interest is what all these results say about the future of institutional investor. Also, how have some of these institutions changed because of the results of these studies? Moreover, the implication of these studies tend to give greater evidence to the random walk and efficient market theories; this is amplified in the concluding chapter.

5 Summary and Conclusions

The purpose of this book has been to study and to evaluate the performance of institutional investors. Particular emphasis has been placed upon pension funds. By applying risk and return, it has been shown that, in most cases, institutional investors have performed more poorly than an unmanaged portfolio with similar risk would have performed. There were a few exceptions to this general conclusion. These exceptions, however, did not occur consistently and, in all probability, were due to chance.

The funds included in this study were bank-administered pension funds, mutual funds, life insurance companies, property and liability insurance companies, and independent investment advisors. Most of these institutions had particular investment goals that were highly unrealistic. In fact, during the late 1960s and early 1970s it was not uncommon for the administrators of these funds to advise their clients that a return of 15 percent was a reasonable expectation of yield on long-term equity investment. When questioned, these institutional investors categorically denied that the return on their investments would not surpass the return on the market in general. A commonly held objective was a minimum 2-4 percent return above the market. In formulating these objectives, virtually no consideration was given to risk.

Based upon the results presented in this study, the above-stated goals proved to be highly unrealistic and unattainable. The fact that these dominant institutions did not outperform an unmanaged portfolio of similar risk indicates a possible misallocation of financial resources. The unexpectedly poor performance of these funds has forced the financial community to appreciate more soberly the potential rewards of equity investing, while evaluating more realistically its inherent risks. The reeducation of institutional investors in the concepts of risk and return is of immeasurable benefit to these financial markets.

One reasonable explanation for the fact that institutions cannot outperform the market on a risk-adjusted basis lies in the existence of an efficient market. No groups of individuals or institutions control the market. The requirements for an efficient market include:

1. Prices must be efficient.
2. Information must be disseminated freely and quickly.
3. Transaction costs must be low enough that investors can earn a net profit from wise investments after all transaction costs.
4. Investors must be rational.[1]

An efficient financial market is highly desirable, and the fact that our markets are efficient puts them in a very advantageous position. Because of this, it is very difficult, if not impossible, to out-perform the market averages consistently when risk is considered.

Random Walk Theory

The apparent inability of well-staffed institutions to out-perform the market may further be explained by the random walk theory. This hypothesis assumes the existence of efficient markets. It purports that (1) successive price changes are independent, and (2) the price changes conform to some probability distribution.[2] In short, the random walk theory states:

> ... that at any given moment in time, the next period price change is random with respect to the state of knowledge at this moment ... and that the current price fully reflects the present state of knowledge in the sense that it is equal to the [discounted] mean value of the distribution of the next period price as given by the present state of knowledge.[3]

In short, all present information is reflected in the price of the stock today, while new information is unpredictable and occurs in a random fashion. As a result, stock prices cannot be predicted.

The findings of this study confirm and support both the concept of efficient markets and the random walk theory. It is also clear that over the last several years, these same findings have been utilized by a growing segment of the investment community. The recent statement by a vice-president of a major brokerage concern supports this observation: "Too much time is being spent on guessing where and when the popular averages will bottom out."[4] This statement characterizes the growing recognition of the futility of predicting stock price changes. Further evidence of this more realistic understanding of the random nature of the stock market is advanced by the American Telephone and Telegraph Company, which now expects and is satisfied with earning a slightly lower equity return on its $10 billion pension portfolio than the Standard and Poor's 500 Stock Index.[5]

One consequence of this new understanding of performance has been the introduction of funds whose aim is to match the return of a broad-based market index. Investment strategy directed at matching market return and minimizing transaction costs appears to have become the sensible manner with which to proceed.

Index-type Mutual Fund

The American Express Company recently introduced an index type mutual fund known as the Index Fund of America.[6] The fund's general goal is to match the performance of the Standard and Poor's 500 Stock Index. It was designed to appeal to institutions, and to pension funds in particular. One attraction of this fund is its variable management fee—when assets exceed $100 million, the management fee will be 1/4 percent, a rate considerably less than that which mutual funds now charge. Wells Fargo Bank and Batterymarch Financial Management Corporation have established similar index-type funds with varying degrees of success.[7]

The establishment of the index-type fund represents the first practical application of the random walk theory, which until recently was popular only among academicians and economists. Several banks have now followed suit by unofficially structuring corporate pension assets to mirror the composition of the Standard and Poor's 500 Stock Index.[8] These moves appear to be a direct consequence of the banks' acceptance of the studies that found their performance to be generally not superior to, and in some instances notably inferior to, the market on a risk-adjusted basis.

Money Market Mutual Fund

In recent years mutual funds have experienced net redemptions of their shares. This has been due to several major factors—overzealous performance expectations, relatively poor performance results, and a generally depressed stock market. In recognition of investor disenchantment with equity mutual funds, the fund industry has responded with short-term money market funds. These mutual funds, generally no-load, are invested in short-term money market instruments such as certificates of deposit, treasury bills, and commercial paper. In 1974 these funds performed impressively, yielding between 9 and 12 percent. It is estimated that as of the end of 1974, there was approximately $3 billion in these money market-type mutual funds.[9] Confidence in this new type of fund was demonstrated by the significant flow of money received during a period of rapidly declining short-term interest rates.[10] These funds represent the industry's innovative response to a fluid economic and financial environment.

Many analyses of mutual funds fail to recognize adequately one particular benefit of these funds. That is, they provide for the smaller investor an opportunity to participate in a diversified stock portfolio with an investment as small as $1,000. Only when a portfolio is fully diversified will the investor avoid unsystematic or avoidable risk. According to modern portfolio theory, the stock market rewards only systematic or market risk, not unsystematic risk. An undiversified portfolio maintains diversifiable risk for which the portfolio is not rewarded.[11]

Obviously, the mutual fund industry should stop trying to emphasize imagined superior stock performance to attract customers. The industry's main asset, and indeed a very real one, is its ability to give investors the opportunity to participate in a fully diversified portfolio of common stocks, thereby minimizing the avoidable risk to the investor as well as minimizing risk for a given rate of return.

Pension Fund Performance

One of the possible effects of the less than optimum investment performance results of bank-administered pension funds will be increased competition for assets. Since a majority of these funds are administered by the 50 largest banks, and since these banks have not performed well in the last several years, it is possible that smaller regional banks may make gains at the expense of these larger city banks.[12] A dramatic example of the type of large-bank results that may increase competition is the performance of the pooled pension equity funds administered by the Morgan Guaranty Trust Company. For the fiscal year ending September 30, 1974, the mean equity return was a whopping –50 percent.[13] Further analysis indicates that between 65 and 70 percent of the pension assets were invested in common stocks. Results of this sort will probably give the smaller banks, which might not invest as heavily in equities, a temporary competitive advantage for the pension dollar.

Competition

The decentralization of pension reserves has also proven advantageous for the independent investment advisor. Generally, investment advisors are viewed as being more flexible in their investment management than are other administrators.[14] The trend toward competition for pension reserves has been accelerating in the 1970s. Due to the new pension reform law and the costs generated by it, this trend will definitely continue. Another tendency which is becoming more apparent is the multiple administration of pension assets. By the end of 1973 the $10 billion American Telephone and Telegraph pension fund had 31 different administrators.[15] The results for each administrator are compared with those of the other fund managers. Such competition will continue, resulting in a further decentralization of reserves.

Pension fund investors must realize that the advisability of maintaining 70 percent of total assets in equities at a time when high-grade corporate bonds are yielding 9-10 percent is, at best, questionable. Although it is true that, for extended periods during the last 50 years, equity returns were greater than those earned on debt, one must not assume that this trend is inalterable. The 9.3 percent equity return found by Lawrence Fisher and J.H. Lorie for the 1926-65 period would undoubtedly be surpassed today if pension funds were invested in quality corporate bonds.[16] Long-term investors must not fail to recognize the greater risk involved in equity investment.

In the future institutional investors must remain sufficiently flexible in order to adapt their investments to the changing economic and financial environment. This flexibility is particularly critical to pension funds, since these funds are especially affected by inflation, increased benefit payments and changes in vesting and funding requirements. The outcome of pension fund investment affects not only the financial markets, but also millions of beneficiaries who are dependent upon these funds. The challenge of responsible investment management must be fully met and understood.

Notes

Notes

Chapter 1
Introduction

1. "Shareholders Total in U.S. Decline Again in '73," *Wall Street Journal*, March 22, 1974, p. 3.

2. "Institutions Widen Stake on Big Board," *New York Times*, March 22, 1974, p. 59.

3. Ibid.

4. "Shareholders Total in U.S. Decline Again in '73," *Wall Street Journal*, March 22, 1974, p. 3; U.S., Congress, Senate, Subcommittee on Financial Markets of the Senate Finance Committee, *The Stockholders Investment Act of 1974*, February 5-6, 1974. Hearing statement by Edward Malca, 93rd Cong., 1st sess., 1974.

5. U.S., Congress, Senate, Subcommittee on Financial Markets of the Senate Finance Committee, *The Impact of Institutional Investors in the Stock Market*, Part 1, July 24-26, 1973 and Part 2, October 24, 25, 27, 28, 1973. 93rd Cong., 1st sess., 1973. Hereafter cited as *Financial Markets Part 1 or 2.*

6. *The Stockholders Investment Act of 1974*, February 5-6, 1974. For a full discussion, see *The Stockholders Investment Act of 1974*, Hearings.

7. "Institutions Widen Stake on Big Board," *New York Times*, March 22, 1974, p. 59.

8. In recent portfolio theory, the need for and the advantages of a well-diversified portfolio have been strongly stressed. The smaller investor is generally not able to diversify his stock portfolio but can definitely do it with as little as $1,000 in mutual funds.

9. New York Stock Exchange, Research Report, *Institutional Holdings of NYSE-listed Stock*, 1970 through 1973, New York.

10. Ibid.

11. *Stockholders Investment Act of 1974*, Hearings, Statement by Edward Malca, p. 99.

12. *Financial Markets*, Part 1, July 24, 1973, Statement by Samuel R. Callaway, p. 68.

13. Federal Deposit Insurance Corporation, *Trust Assets of Insured Commercial Banks*, Washington, D.C., 1973.

14. For a thought-provoking discussion of the need for full

institutional disclosure, see John P. Wheeler III, "The Institutional Investor Disclosure Act: An Analysis of the Consumer Benefits," *The Yale Law Journal*, May 1974, pp. 1271-90.

15. *Financial Markets*, Part 2, p. 7.

16. *Financial Markets*, Part 2, p. 99, Statement by Senator Lloyd Bentsen. The two banks mentioned were Morgan Guaranty Trust and Bankers Trust.

17. Ibid., p. 100.

18. *Financial Markets*, Part 2, p. 1.

19. *Financial Markets*, Part 2, p. 20, Statement by Dr. Norman B. Ture.

20. *Financial Markets*, Part 2, p. 34, Statement by Dr. Richard A. Musgrove.

21. Robert M. Soldofsky, *Institutional Holdings of Common Stocks 1900-2000* (Ann Arbor, Michigan: Bureau of Business Research, Graduate School of Business Administration, University of Michigan, 1971), p. 209.

Chapter 2
Goals and Objectives of Institutional Investors

1. Donaldson, Lufkin and Jenrette, Inc., *6th Annual Corporate Pension Conference*, November 1969, New York, New York.

2. Ibid., p. 38.

3. Ibid., pp. 29-30.

4. Donaldson, Lufkin and Jenrette, Inc., *7th Annual Corporate Pension Conference*, November 1970, New York, New York.

5. Ibid., p. 41.

6. Ibid.

7. Title Insurance and Trust Company, *Annual Report of Pooled Funds for Employee Benefit Plans, 1970*, p. 6.

8. First Minneapolis Bank, *Annual Report of the Collective Funds for Employee Benefit Plans, 1970*, p. 18.

9. For a fascinating account of that period, see *The Go-Go Years* (New York: John Brooks, Weybright and Talley, 1973).

10. "Rating the Money Managers," *Barron's*, October 22, 1973, p. 3.

11. "Bye-Bye, Go-Go?," *Wall Street Journal*, June 7, 1973, p. 1.

12. Ibid.

13. Securities and Exchange Commission, "Private Noninsured Pension Funds 1973," *Statistical Bulletin*, (Washington, D.C., 1974), p. 455.

14. Ibid.

15. Ibid.

16. Standard and Poor's/Inter Capital, Inc., *Third Annual Pension Fund Management Survey*, November 1973 (New York, 1973).

17. Securities and Exchange Commission, "Private Noninsured Pension Funds 1964," *Statistical Series # 2053*, p. 1-6; Securities and Exchange Commission, "Private Noninsured Pension Funds 1972," *Statistical Bulletin*, 1973, p. 867.

18. Robert D. Paul, "Can Private Pension Plans Deliver," *Harvard Business Review*, September-October 1974, pp. 22-24.

19. It seems very likely that if inflation continues above 10 percent for a sustained period, then the private pension system will not be able to support fully the necessary new benefit levels. The pension system would then have to change dramatically.

20. See "The New Pension Law May Cut Profits Less Than First Thought," *Wall Street Journal*, October 1, 1974, p. 1.

21. Ibid.; Thomas, Dana L., "Escalating Pensions," *Barron's*, March 18, 1974, p. 3.

22. *Wall Street Journal*, October 1, 1974, p. 1.

23. Employment Retirement Income Security Act of 1974, Public Law 93-406, 93rd Cong., H.R. 2, September 2, 1974.

24. "Pension Reform Casts a Giant Shadow," *New York Times*, August 18, 1974, p. 12.

25. "Pension Reform Bill Signed by President," *New York Times*, September 3, 1974, p. 1.

26. Estimated by Steven Lewins, research director of Arnold Bernhard and Co., as quoted in *Wall Street Journal*, October 1, 1974, p. 18.

27. Ibid.

28. Ibid.

29. "Rating Money Managers," *Barron's*, October 22, 1973, p. 3.

30. For an interesting discussion of this point, see "Escalating Pensions," *Barron's*, March 18, 1974, p. 3.

31. Standard and Poor's/Inter Capital, Inc., *Third Annual Pension Management Survey*, November 1973 (New York, 1973).

32. "Escalating Pensions," *Barron's*, March 18, 1974, p. 14.

33. Lawrence Fisher and J.H. Lorie, "Rates of Return on Investments in Common Stock: The Year-by-Year Record, 1926-1965," *Journal of Business*, July 1968, pp. 291-316.

34. "Market Place," *New York Times*, July 18, 1974.

35. A 1 percent commission charge is assumed in this calculation.

36. For the most recent performance data, see "Corporate Sales of Bonds to Public Rose to Record in '74," *New York Times*, January 30, 1975, p. 17.

37. Salomon Brothers, *1973 Annual Review of the Bond Market* (New York, 1974), pp. 4-5.

38. *Wall Street Journal*, July 2, 1974.

Chapter 3
Performance Studies

1. *Institutional Investor*, July 1974, p. 65.

2. Ibid.

3. A.G. Becker and Company is an investment firm that specializes in conducting pension performance studies.

4. *Institutional Investor*, July 1974, p. 65.

5. Ibid.

6. Ibid., p. 66.

7. Irwin Friend, Marshall Blume, and Jean Crockett, *Mutual Funds and Other Institutional Investors: A New Prospective* (New York: McGraw-Hill, 1970), p. 4.

8. Much of this section is based upon Edward Malca, *Bank-Administered, Commingled Pension Funds: Performance and Characteristics 1962-1970* (Lexington, Mass.: Lexington Books, D.C. Heath and Co., 1973), pp. 27-31.

9. See, for example, Malca, *Pension Funds*, and Securities and Exchange Commission, *Institutional Investor Study Report*, vol. 2 (Washington, D.C.: U.S. Government Printing Office, 1971); Friend et al., *Mutual Funds.*

10. Harry Markowitz, "Portfolio Selection," *Journal of Finance* March 1952, pp. 77-91; idem., *Portfolio Selection* (New York: John Wiley, 1959).

11. Markowitz, *Portfolio Selection*, p. 100, fn.

12. William F. Sharpe, "A Simplified Model for Portfolio Analysis," *Management Science*, vol. 9, no. 1, 1963, pp. 277-93.

13. The proxy for the riskless rate of return is the 90-day treasury bill rate.

14. See Jack L. Treynor, "How to Rate Management of Investment Funds," *Harvard Business Review*, vol. 43, January-February, 1965, pp. 63-75; Sharpe, "Simplified Model"; Securities and Exchange Commission, *Study*, p. 400; Michael C. Jensen, "The Performance of Mutual Funds in the Period 1945-1964," *Journal of Finance*, Vol. 23, May 1968, pp. 389-416.

15. Jensen, "Performance of Mutual Funds."

16. It was found that on average the rate of return of these funds was inferior to an unmanaged portfolio of similar risk.

17. Jensen, "Performance of Mutual Funds."

18. Securities and Exchange Commission, *Study*, vol. 2; Malca, *Pension Funds*; Friend et al., *Mutual Funds.*

19. Steven C. Leuthold, *Perception Indices* (Minneapolis, Minnesota: Capital Market Systems, 1974).

20. Ibid., p. 6.

21. Ibid., p. 7.

22. Ibid.

23. Ibid.

24. For a thorough discussion of the weighting procedure and rationale used, see Ibid., pp. 7-8.

25. The possibility of index funds as a possible investment alternative is discussed in Chapter 4.

26. For example: Callan Associates, Inc., San Francisco, California; A.G. Becker and Company, New York; Merrill, Lynch, Pierce, Fenner and Smith, New York.

27. Friend et al., *Mutual Funds*, p. 60.

28. See Malca, *Pension Funds*, pp. 49-50.

29. Ibid.

30. The mean beta coefficient for the five-year period ending June 30, 1974, is 1.06 for Group I and 1.01 for Group II.

31. See, for example, Jerome B. Cohen, Edward Zinbarg, and Arthur Zeikel, *Investment Analysis and Portfolio Management* (Homewood, Illinois: Richard D. Irwin, 1973), pp. 737-91.

32. There are 31 funds in Group I and 27 funds in Group II.

33. This general finding tends to go against most other findings of institutional investor performance: See Malca, *Pension Funds*; Jensen, "Mutual Fund Performance"; Securities and Exchange Commission, *Study*; Friend et al., *Mutual Funds.*

34. A similar relationship was found for mutual funds; see Marshall Blume and Irwin Friend, "Measurement of Portfolio Performance Under Uncertainty," *American Economic Review*, September 1970, pp. 561-75.

35. Ibid. For an interesting discussion of possible explanations.

36. Malca, *Pension Funds.*

37. "Rating the Money Managers," *Barron's*, October 22, 1973, p. 3.

38. See Table 3-4.

39. See, for example, "Bye-Bye, Go-Go?," *Wall Street Journal*, June 7, 1973, p. 1.

40. See R.A. Brealey, *An Introduction to Risk and Return from Common Stocks* (Cambridge, Massachusetts: M.I.T., 1969); Paul Cootner, ed., *The Random Character of Stock Prices* (Cambridge, Massachusetts: M.I.T., 1964).

41. Malca, *Pension Funds*; idem., "Bank Fund Performance," *Commercial and Financial Chronicle*, August 23, 1973, p. 1.

42. Securities and Exchange Commission (SEC), *Study*, vol. 2, pp. 400-10.

43. Malca, *Pension Funds*, pp. 42-43.

44. Similar results were obtained by the SEC, *Study*, and Friend et al., *Mutual Funds.*

45. For similar findings, see SEC, *Study*, vol. 2; Friend et al., *Mutual Funds.*

46. Blume and Friend, "Measurement," pp. 561-75.

47. Malca, *Pension Funds*, found that this relationship was not true for intraperiod 1962-65 but was true for both 1962-70 and the intraperiod 1966-70. Blume and Friend, "Measurement," found similar results.

48. In the later part of this chapter a thorough analysis of recent New York City bank performance is discussed.

49. U.S., Congress, Senate, Subcommittee on Financial Markets of the Finance Committee, *Stockholders Investors Act of 1974*, February 5-6, 1974, Hearing statements by Edward Malca, Samuel Calloway, and George Lingua, 93rd Cong., 2nd sess., 1974.

50. "Market Place," *New York Times*, April 23, 1974, p. 56.

51. See Malca, *Pension Funds*, pp. 42-43; also the Callan Associates Study discussed in the earlier part of this chapter.

52. U.S., Congress, *Stockholders Investors Act of 1974*, Statement by George M. Lingua, February 5, 1974.

53. This result has also been found for many other institutional investors. See SEC, *Institutional Investor Study;* Friend et al., *Mutual Funds;* Malca, *Pension Funds.* The recent performance results of the Morgan Guaranty Trust Company's pooled equity funds for employee benefit plans are as follows:

	Rate of Return Fiscal Year Ending 9/30/74
Special equity fund	–55.1%
Intermediate capitalization fund	–49.7%
Common stock fund	–44.6%
Standard & Poor's 500 Stock Index	–39.0%

Note: All results include reinvestment of dividends.
Source: "Heard on the Street," *Wall Street Journal*. December 9, 1974, p. 35.

54. Statement by Bradford F. Story, senior partner of the investment firm of Brundage, Story and Rose. Statement appeared in "Market Place," *New York Times*, January 24, 1974, p. 50. ©1974 by The New York Times Company. Reprinted by permission.

55. *TIAA-CREF, 1973*, Teachers Insurance and Annuity Association–College Retirement Equities Fund (New York, 1974), p. 7.

56. There are larger retirement funds, such as the pension fund of the American Telephone and Telegraph Company. These funds, however, are managed by numerous outside advisors.

57. From an interview with James Farrel, Jr., investment officer of TIAA-CREF, June 19, 1974.

Chapter 4
Other Institutional Performance

1. Dreher, Roger and Associates, *Investment Performance* (New York, 1974).

2. Some recent mutual fund studies are the following: William F. Sharpe, "Mutual Fund Performance," *Journal of Business*, vol. 39, pt. 2, January 1966, pp. 119-38; Michael Jensen, "The Performance of Mutual Funds in the Period 1945-1964," *Journal of Finance*, vol. 23, May 1968, pp. 386-416; SEC, *Institutional Investor Study*, vol. 2, 1971, pp. 139-399; Irwin Friend, Marshall Blume, and Jean

Crockett, *Mutual Funds and Other Institutional Investors: A New Perspective* (New York: McGraw-Hill, 1970).

3. The Securities and Exchange Commission, *Investment Trusts and Investment Companies Part I*, (Washington, D.C.: U.S. Government Printing Office, 1939), p. 492.

4. *A Study of Mutual Funds*, prepared for the Securities and Exchange Commission by the Wharton School of Finance and Commerce, (Washington, D.C.: U.S. Government Printing Office, 1962), p. 297.

5. Ibid.

6. Friend et al., *Mutual Funds.*

7. Jensen, "Mutual Fund Performance," p. 415.

8. Ibid, p. 406.

9. Ibid., p. 410

10. Securities and Exchange Commission, *Study*, vol. 6, pp. 19-33.

11. Ibid., p. 31.

12. Wiesenberger Services, Inc., *Mutual Fund Performance Monthly, January, 1974*, (New York, 1974).

13. Dividends and capital appreciation are included in both calculations.

14. Chapter 3 thoroughly discussed this fact.

15. Wiesenberger, *Mutual Fund Performance*, p. 34.

16. Securities and Exchange Commission, *Study*, vol. 8, p. 47.

17. *Life Insurance Fact Book*, Institute of Life Insurance (New York, 1974), p. 77.

18. Securities and Exchange Commission, *Study*, vol. 2, pp. 735-45.

19. See Ibid, Chapters IV and V for mutual fund and bank-managed collective fund performance; Edward Malca, *Bank-Administered, Commingled Pension Funds: Performance and Characteristics 1962-1970* (Lexington, Mass.: Lexington Books, D.C. Heath and Co., 1973), p. 48.

20. Securities and Exchange Commission, *Study*, vol. 2, p. 742.

21. Callan Associates, *Performance Study* (San Francisco, California 1974), p. 3.

22. See Table 3-7 in Chapter 3 for further details.

23. Alfred M. Best & Co., *Best's Fire and Casualty Aggregates and Averages* (New York, 1974).

24. Gary Schlarbaum, "The Investment Performance of the Common Stock Portfolio of Property-Liability Companies," *Journal of Financial and Quantitative Analysis*, January 1974, pp. 89-106.

25. Ibid., p. 92.

26. Ibid., p. 98.

27. It was often found that when the gross basis was used for mutual fund studies their performance was equivalent to the comparison standard.

28. Schlarbaum, "Investment Performance," p. 101. Reprinted with permission.

29. Generally considered to include charitable, religious, educational, civic, social, and eleemosynary organizations exempt from federal taxation under Section 5 of the Internal Revenue Code.

30. The Ford Foundation, *Managing Educational Endowments* (New York, August 1969), p. 3.

31. Jerome Cohen, Edward Zinbarg, and Arthur Zeikel, *Investment Analysis and Portfolio Management* (New York: McGraw-Hill, 1973), p. 727.

32. This definition was taken from a study by the New York Stock Exchange entitled, *Non-Profit Institutions–Their Role as Institutional Investors*, September 1968.

33. Estimated by Hayden Smith of the Council for Financial Aid to Education, quoted in *Business Week*, December 26, 1970, p. 44.

34. Estimated by the *Money Market Directory* (New York, 1972), p. iii.

35. Annual survey of *35 Leading University Endowments*, by Stillman, Maynard and Co. (New York, 1972).

36. *Wall Street Journal*, April 25, 1974, p. 1.

37. "Market Place," *New York Times*, April 11, 1974, p. 50.

38. The Ford Foundation, *Managing Educational Endowments*, pp. 45-47.

39. Ibid., p. 3.

40. Ibid., pp. 3-4.

41. Ibid., p. 57.

42. Ibid. Note that the University of Rochester is shown separately because it is a well-known example of an educational institution that 20 years ago adopted the objective of long-term growth for most of its endowment fund (p. 57).

43. J. Peter Williamson, *Performance Measurement and Investment Objectives for Educational Endowment Funds* (Ford Foundation, April 1972).

44. The two studies are The Ford Foundation, *Managing Educational Endowments;* Williamson, *Performance Measurement.*

45. However, it is quite likely that since June 30, 1971, these

educational endowment funds have significantly increased their portfolio risk in order to maximize total return. Thus, this criticism of an overly conservative investment policy is not warranted today.

46. One contributing factor is that foundation assets are stated at book value, which is not useful for performance measurement.

Chapter 5
Summary and Conclusions

1. Jack Francis *Investments: Analysis and Management* (New York: McGraw-Hill, 1972), p. 53.
2. Eugene F. Fama, "The Behavior of Stock Market Prices," *Journal of Business*, January 1965, p. 35.
3. O.A. Vasicek and J.A. McQuown, "Efficient Market Model," *Financial Analysts Journal*, vol. 28, no. 5, 1972, p. 76.
4. Statement by Marshall Acuff, Jr., vice-president of Smith Barney and Company, in "Heard on the Street," *Wall Street Journal*, July 23, 1974, p. 41.
5. "Market Place," *New York Times*, July 4, 1974, p. 26.
6. It was introduced in early 1974.
7. For an interesting article on index funds, see "Bye-Bye, Go-Go?", *Wall Street Journal*, June 7, 1973, p. 1.
8. Ibid.
9. *Wall Street Journal*, "Interest Rates for Short Term Decline Sharply," December 10, 1974, p. 36.
10. *Wall Street Journal*, "Money Market Funds Say Sales Surged in January Despite Slide of Interest Rates," February 3, 1975, p. 20.
11. James Lorie and Mary Hamilton, *The Stock Market: Theories and Evidence* (Homewood, Illinois: Richard D. Irwin, 1973), p. 254.
12. An interesting article that discusses this trend is "Have Regional Banks Really Penetrated the National Pension Market?", *Institutional Investor*, July 1974, p. 292.
13. "Heard on the Street," *Wall Street Journal*, December 9, 1974, p. 35.
14. For an interesting discussion on this point, see "Heard on the Street," *Wall Street Journal*, January 17, 1975, p. 29.
15. "Market Place," *New York Times*, February 23, 1974, p. 40.
16. L. Fisher, and James Lorie, "Rates of Return on Investments in Common Stocks: Year-by-Year Record," *Journal of Business*, July 1968, p. 296.

Bibliography

Bibliography

Books

Aber, John. *Beta Coefficient and Models of Security Returns.* Lexington, Mass.: Lexington Books, D.C. Heath and Co., 1973.

Brealey, R.A. *An Introduction to Risk and Return from Common Stocks.* Cambridge, Mass.: M.I.T. Press, 1969.

Brooks, John. *The Go-Go Years.* New York: Weybright and Talley, 1973.

Cohen, Jerome; Zinbarg, Edward; and Zeikel, Arthur. *Investment Analysis and Portfolio Management.* Homewood, Illinois: Richard D. Irwin, 1973.

Cootner, Paul, ed. *The Random Character of Stock Prices.* Cambridge, Mass.: M.I.T. Press, 1964.

Ellis, Charles D. *Institutional Investing.* Homewood, Illinois: Richard D. Irwin, 1971.

Francis, Jack. *Investments: Analysis and Management.* New York: McGraw-Hill, 1972.

Friend, Irwin; Blume, Marshall; and Crockett, Jean. *Mutual Funds and Other Institutional Investors, a New Perspective.* New York: McGraw-Hill, 1970.

Harbrecht, Paul. *Pension Funds and Economic Power.* New York: Twentieth Century Fund, 1959.

Jensen, Michael C., ed. *Studies in the Theory of Capital Markets.* New York: Praeger Press, 1972.

Lorie, James, and Hamilton, Mary. *The Stock Market: Theories and Evidence.* Homewood, Illinois: Richard D. Irwin, 1973.

Malca, Edward. *Bank-Administered, Commingled Pension Funds: Performance and Characteristics 1962-1970.* Lexington, Massachusetts: Lexington Books, D.C. Heath and Co., 1973.

Malkiel, Burton. *A Random Walk Down Wall Street.* New York: W.W. Norton, 1973.

Managing Educational Endowments. New York: The Ford Foundation, 1969.

Markowitz, Harry. *Portfolio Selection.* New York: John Wiley, 1959.

Money Market Directory. New York: 1972. Money Market Directories, Inc.

Murray, Roger F. *Economic Aspects of Pensions: Summary Report.*

New York: National Bureau of Economic Research, Columbia University Press, 1968.

Soldofsky, Robert M. *Institutional Holdings of Common Stocks 1900-2000.* Ann Arbor, Michigan: Bureau of Business Research, Graduate School of Business Administration, The University of Michigan, 1971.

Williamson, J. Peter. *Performance Measurement and Investment Objectives for Educational Endowment Funds.* New York: The Common Fund, 1972.

Journals and Periodicals

"Escalating Pension." *Barron's.* March 18, 1974, p. 3. "Rating the Money Managers." *Barron's.* October 22, 1973, p. 3.

Bernstein, Peter L. "What Rate of Return Can You Really Expect?" *Journal of Finance*, May 1973.

Blume, M.E. and Friend, I. "A New Look at The Capital Asset Pricing Model." *Journal of Finance*, March 1973, pp. 1-10; 19-33.

________. "Measurement of Portfolio Performance Under Uncertainty." *American Economic Review*, September 1970, pp. 561-75.

Blume, M.E. "On the Assessment of Risk." *Journal of Finance*, March 1971.

Business Week. December 26, 1970, p. 44.

Fama, Eugene F. "The Behavior of Stock Market Prices." *Journal of Business*, January 1965, pp. 34-105.

Fisher, Lawrence and Lorie, James. "Rates of Return on Investments in Common Stocks: Year-by-Year Record." *Journal of Business*, July 1968, pp. 291-316.

Grier, Paul C. "Large Block Trades and Price Behavior of NYSE Listed Stocks." *Journal of Business*, July 1973, pp. 425-33.

Hartwell, J.M. "Performance: Its Promise and Problems." *Financial Analysts Journal*, March-April 1969, pp. 115-117.

"Have Regional Banks Really Penetrated the National Pension Market?" *Institutional Investor*, July 1974, pp. 71-84.

Jensen, Michael. "Risk, the Pricing of Capital Assets and the Evaluation of Investment Portfolios." *Journal of Business*, April 1969, pp. 167-247.

_______. "The Performance of Mutual Funds in the Period 1945-1964." *Journal of Finance*, May 1968, pp. 389-416.

Katz, Steven. "The Price Adjustment Process of Bonds to Rating Reclassifications: A Test of Bond Market Efficiency." *Journal of Finance*, May 1974, pp. 551-59.

Levy, R.A. "Measurement of Investment Performance." *Journal of Financial and Quantitative Analysis* 3, no. 1 (1968), pp. 35-57.

_______. "What Price Performance?" *Barron's*, July 5, 1971, pp. 11-14.

Malca, Edward. "Pension Fund Performance." *The Commercial and Financial Chronicle*, August 23, 1973, pp. 1-4.

Markowitz, Harry. "Portfolio Selection." *Journal of Finance*, March 1952, pp. 77-91.

McDonald, John. "French Mutual Fund Performance: Evaluation of Internationally-Diversified Portfolios." *Journal of Finance*, December 1973, pp. 1161-80.

Paul, Robert D. "Can Private Pension Plans Deliver." *Harvard Business Review*, September-October 1974, pp. 22-24.

Pogue, Gerald A. and Modigliani, Franco. "An Introduction to Risk and Return: Concepts and Evidence Parts I and II." *Financial Analysts Journal*, March-April and May-June 1974, pp. 68-70 and 69-85.

Schlarbaum, Gary. "The Investment Performance of the Common Stock Portfolio of Property-Liability Companies." *Journal of Financial and Quantitative Analysis*, January 1974, pp. 89-106.

Sharpe, William F. "A Simplified Model for Portfolio Analysis." *Management Science*, January 1963, pp. 277-93.

_______. "Mutual Fund Performance." *Journal of Business* 39, pt. 2 (January 1966), pp. 119-38.

_______. "Portfolio Analysis." *Journal of Financial Quantitative Analysis*, June 1967, pp. 76-84.

Spigelman, J.H. "What Basis For Superior Performance?" *Financial Analysts Journal*, May-June 1974, pp. 32-34.

Treynor, Jack L. and Mazuy, Kay K. "Can Mutual Funds Outguess the Market?" *Harvard Business Review*, July-August 1966, pp. 131-36.

Treynor, Jack L. "How to Rate Management of Investment Funds." *Harvard Business Review*, January-February 1965, pp. 63-75.

Vasicek, O.A. and McQuown, J.A. "Efficient Market Model." *Financial Analysts Journal*, 28, no. 5 (1972), pp. 71-84.

Wheeler III, John P. "The Institutional Investor Disclosure Act: An Analysis of the Consumer Benefits." *The Yale Law Journal*, May 1974, pp. 1271-90.

Newspapers

"Corporate Sales of Bonds to Public Rose to Record in '74." *New York Times.* January 30, 1975, p. 17.
"Institutions Widen Stake on Big Board." *New York Times.* March 22, 1974, p. 3.
"Market Place." *New York Times.* July 18, 1974, p. 49.
"Market Place." *New York Times*, July 4, 1974, p. 26.
"Market Place." *New York Times.* April 23, 1974, p. 52.
"Market Place." *New York Times.* April 11, 1974.
"Market Place." *New York Times.* February 23, 1974, p. 40.
"Market Place." *New York Times.* January 24, 1974, p. 50.
"Pension Reform Bill Signed by President." *New York Times.* September 3, 1974, p. 1.
"Pension Reform Casts a Giant Shadow." *New York Times.* August 18, 1974, p. 12.
Wall Street Journal. April 25, 1974, p. 1.
"Bye-Bye, Go-Go?" *Wall Street Journal.* June 7, 1973, p. 1.
"Heard on the Street." *Wall Street Journal.* January 17, 1975, p. 29.
"Heard on the Street." *Wall Street Journal.* December 9, 1974, p. 35.
"Heard on the Street." *Wall Street Journal.* July 23, 1974, p. 41.
"Money Market Funds Say Sales Surged in January Despite Slide of Interest Rates." *Wall Street Journal.* February 3, 1975, p. 20.
"Shareholders Total in U.S. Decline Again in '73." *Wall Street Journal.* March 22, 1974, p. 3.
"The New Pension Law May Cut Profits Less Than First Thought." *Wall Street Journal.* October 1, 1974, p. 1.

Reports and Unpublished Papers

Annual Report of Pooled Funds for Employee Benefit Plans, 1970. Minneapolis, Minn.: First Minneapolis Bank, 1971.
Annual Report of Pooled Funds for Employee Benefit Plans, 1970. Los Angeles, Calif.: Title Insurance and Trust Company, 1971.
Best's Fire and Casualty Aggregates and Averages. New York: Alfred M. Best and Company, 1974.
Donaldson, Lufkin and Jenrette, Inc. *Seventh and Sixth Annual Pension Conference Summary of Proceedings.* New York, 1969 and 1970.

Institutional Holdings of NYSE-Listed Stocks. 1970, 1971, 1972, and 1973. New York: The New York Stock Exchange. 1971-74.

Investment Performance. New York: Dreher, Roger and Associates, 1974.

Leuthold, Steven C., *Perception Indices.* Minneapolis, Minn.: Capital Market Systems, 1974.

Life Insurance Fact Book. New York: Institute of Life Insurance, 1974.

Malca, Edward, "Noninsured Private Pension Funds as an Institutional Investor." New York: Baruch College, 1969.

Mutual Fund Performance Monthly, January, 1974. New York: Wiesenberger Services, Inc., 1974.

1974 Fact Book. New York: The New York Stock Exchange, June 1974.

1973 Annual Review of the Bond Market. New York: Salomon Brothers, 1974.

Non-Profit Institutions–Their Role as Institutional Investors. New York: The New York Stock Exchange, 1968.

Reports II and III of the Trust and Investment Division. New York: Morgan Guaranty Trust Company, 1973 and 1974.

Standard and Poor's/Inter Capital, Inc., *Third Annual Fund Management Survey.* New York, November 1973.

Summary of Time Weighted Rates of Return Cumulative Periods Ending June 30, 1974. San Francisco, Calif.: Callan Associates, Inc., 1974.

Survey of 35 Leading University Endowments. New York: Stillman, Maynard and Company, 1972.

TIAA-CREF, 1973. New York: Teachers Insurance and Annuity Association–College Retirement Equities Fund. 1974.

Public Documents

The 100 Largest Retirement Plans 1960-1968. Washington, D.C.: U.S. Government Printing Office, 1969.

The Internal Revenue Code: 1954. Washington, D.C.: U.S. Government Printing Office, 1954.

Employment Retirement Income Security Act of 1974 Public Law 93-406, 93rd Cong., H.R. 2, September 2, 1974.

Federal Deposit Insurance Corporation, *Trust Assets of Insured Commercial Banks.* Washington, D.C., 1973.

Federal Reserve System. *The Federal Reserve Bulletin*, October and December, 1974.

Securities and Exchange Commission. *A Study of Mutual Funds*, prepared by the Wharton School of Finance and Commerce. Washington, D.C.: U.S. Government Printing Office, 1962.

Securities and Exchange Commission. *Institutional Investor Study Report.* Washington, D.C.: U.S. Government Printing Office, 1971.

Securities and Exchange Commission. *Investment Trusts and Investment Companies.* Washington, D.C.: U.S. Government Printing Office, 1939.

Securities and Exchange Commission. *Private Noninsured Pension Funds, 1972 and 1973*, September 1973 and 1974. Washington, D.C., 1974.

Securities and Exchange Commission. *Statistical Bulletin*, August 1973; April and August, 1974. Washington, D.C.: U.S. Government Printing Office, 1973 and 1974.

Securities and Exchange Commission. "Private Noninsured Pension Funds 1964," *Statistical Series # 2053.* Washington, D.C., 1964.

Securities and Exchange Commission. *Stock Transactions of Selected Financial Institutions and Foreigners, 1973*, April 3, 1974. Washington, D.C., 1974.

U.S., Congress, Joint Economic Committee. *Investment Policies of Pension Funds.* Washington, D.C.: U.S. Government Printing Office, 1970.

U.S., Congress, Joint Economic Committee. *Old Age Income Assurance*, pt. IV. Washington, D.C.: U.S. Government Printing Office, 1967.

U.S., Congress, Senate, Committee on Banking and Currency. *Institutional Investors and the Stock Market: 1953-1955.* Washington, D.C.: U.S. Government Printing Office, 1956.

U.S., Congress, Senate, Special Committee on Aging. *Economics of Aging; Toward a Full Share in Abundance, Pts. 10A and 10B Pension Aspects.* 91st Cong., 2nd sess. Washington, D.C.: U.S. Government Printing Office, 1970.

U.S., Congress, Senate, Subcommittee in Financial Markets of the Senate Finance Committee. *The Impact of Institutional Investors in the Stock Market.* 93rd Cong., 1st sess. Washington, D.C.: U.S. Government Printing Office, 1973.

U.S., Congress, Senate, Subcommittee on Financial Markets of the

Senate Finance Committee. *The Stockholders Investment Act of 1974.* 93rd Cong., 1st sess. Washington, D.C.: U.S. Government Printing Office, 1974.

U.S., Congress, Senate, Subcommittee on Intergovernmental Relations of the Committee on Government Operations. *Disclosure of Corporate Ownership.* Washington, D.C.: U.S. Government Printing Office, 1974.

U.S. Department of Commerce. *Business Statistics, 1971.* Washington, D.C.: U.S. Government Printing Office, 1971.

Miscellaneous

Interview with James Farrell, Jr., investment officer of TIAA-CREF. New York, June 19, 1974.

"Methods of Measuring Portfolio Performance." Seminar sponsored by Merrill, Lynch, Pierce, Fenner and Smith, Inc., October 1967.

Index

Index

About the Author

Edward Malca is assistant professor of economics at Richmond College of the City University of New York, where he received the Ph.D. in 1973. Besides his teaching position, Dr. Malca is also president of Malca Investment Advisory Service, a firm that specializes in pension performance and portfolio management evaluation. Furthermore, he has had experience in the research department of a Wall Street investment banking firm. Dr. Malca has testified before the U.S. Senate Finance Committee on Pension and Institutional Investor legislation. He is the author of *Bank-Administered, Commingled Pension Funds: Performance and Characteristics, 1962-1970* (Lexington Books, 1973), and he has contributed to the *Wall Street Journal, The Commercial and Financial Chronicle*, and other professional journals. He is a member of both The American Finance Association and The American Economic Association.